Exploring
STRATHCLYDE
by rail

D0183581

Key to front cover pictures

1 — Electric multiple unit crossing the River Leven at Dumbarton — *Tom Noble*

2 — The Isle of Arran from the Ayrshire coast — *Eric Thorburn/Cunninghame District Council*

3 — Burns cottage, Alloway — *Tom Noble*

4 — The City Chambers, Glasgow — *Greater Glasgow Tourist Board and Convention Bureau*

Exploring
STRATHCLYDE
by rail

by
Tom Noble

with additional walks by
Roger Smith

Edited by Barbara Allen
Series Editor Stan Abbott

Published by Leading Edge Press and Publishing, The Old Chapel, Burtersett, Hawes, North Yorkshire, DL8 3PB.
☎ (0969) 667566

British Library Cataloguing in Publication Data

Noble,Tom
    Exploring Strathclyde by rail. — (RailTrail Series)
    1. Scotland. Strathclyde Region — Visitors' guide
    I. Series
    914.14104858

    ISBN 0-948135-20-4

Designer: Barbara Allen
Sketch maps: Nicholas Bagguley*
Type: Leading Edge Press & Publishing
Colour reprographics: Impression, Leeds
Printed and bound in Great Britain by Ebenezer Baylis and Son Ltd, Worcester
RailTrail series logo by Barbara Drew

Maps are for guidance only and not necessarily to scale.

Contents

Foreword

BY STEPHEN R LOCKLEY
Director General,
Strathclyde Passenger Transport Executive

THIS is an opportune time for production of a book on the Strathclyde rail network and the area it serves. Almost half of Scotland's population resides in the Region, which covers one sixth of the Scottish land area and embraces the full range of urban, rural and island communities.

Glasgow, the heart of the Region, derives its name from "green hollow" and grew at the lowest point where the river Clyde could be bridged. By 1900 the city could justifiably claim to be the second city of the Empire. Strathclyde became a powerhouse of the industrial revolution. In particular, its railway engineering acquired a worldwide reputation only rivalled by its shipbuilding.

The subsequent decline in heavy engineering led to a long period of social and economic deterioration, but the spirit and determination of the residents of Strathclyde has led to a renaissance during the last 20 years or so culminating with Glasgow's year as European City of Culture.

The Region is fortunate in inheriting much of the rail network which grew up during the 19th century. The local network centred on Glasgow is the largest in Britain outside London and serves all the major population centres, as well as the majority of smaller towns.

The Regional Council provides financial support for the network, which amounts to £12 for each of the 2.4 million residents and represents half of the costs incurred. The PTE determines the level of service in accordance with the council's policies.

Major investment has included the reopening of the Argyle line, connecting electric services north and south of the river Clyde in 1979, and electrification of the lines to Ayr and Largs in 1986. Coupled with the comprehensive modernisation of rolling stock and the opening of 25 stations during the last 15 years, the network provides quick accessible travel throughout most of the Region.

The Paisley Canal Line was reopened in 1990 and there are plans to reopen the Glasgow Northern Suburban Line, the Rutherglen-Coatbridge Line and the Larkhall Line.

In Glasgow, the local ScotRail network connects with the famous Underground system, operated by Strathclyde PTE and extensively modernised in the late 1970s. It is one of the earliest underground railways in the world and reputed to be a model for the Paris Metro.

The conurbation was also famed for its trams, and although the last of these ceased to run 30 years ago, they are remembered with nostalgia. Taking account of the increasing demand for travel and recognising that unrestrained road traffic demand cannot be catered for simply by building new roads, plans are afoot to provide the modern equivalent of trams, a light rail system, utilising the versatility of modern technology to reach areas presently not well served by rail.

This book provides comprehensive information on the Region's heritage and how to enjoy it by utilising the rail systems. I commend it to you and am confident that your experience in using the trains will encourage you to make many more excursions.

September 1990

Introduction

Balloch to Airdrie train passes through Bowling on the Firth of Clyde

THERE is much to see and do in Strathclyde and, despite its size, getting around the region is not difficult, thanks to the comprehensive and ever-growing rail network. All the walks in this book can be made using Strathclyde Transport's Day Tripper ticket, which includes rail, underground and most major bus services. The area it covers stretches from Ardlui at the northern end of Loch Lomond, to the south of Girvan on the coast. Also available is a day rover for the Glasgow Underground system which, although restricted in the area it serves, is frequent and speedy.

Industrial museums figure prominently in the list of attractions, as would be expected of an area with a tradition of engineering in all its forms. The Clyde's fame as a shipbuilding centre was worldwide; the phrase Clyde-built became a synonym for quality and it is estimated that in the two centuries of growth from wooden-hulled vessels to the mighty Cunarders — culminating in the *QE2* — some 30,000 ships were built on the river. At the industry's peak there were 70 shipyards on the Clyde — now they can be counted on the fingers of one hand. Alongside shipbuilding grew the marine engineering industry, developments which, especially in the mid-19th century, were reflected in other aspects of steam engineering.

Glasgow — and more particularly its district of Springburn — was the undisputed capital of railway locomotive construction, supplying the Caledonian

Railway, the North British Railway, and other railways at home and abroad wherever the world atlas was coloured pink.

Of course, these industries would have been nothing without the raw material supplied by the iron smelters and later the steelworks, which in turn, like everyone else, were wholly dependent on coal. The mines of Ayrshire and Lanarkshire fed the furnaces and the boilers; new pits spawned new railways and almost every major shipyard or engineering works had its own private sidings. As emigrants from such areas as Ireland and the Highlands swarmed into the burgeoning industrial centres, transporting people became almost as important as moving materials, and the rail network as we know it today was born.

In view of this background of engineering, it is perhaps slightly ironic that the finest monument to the area's industrial past has its roots in textiles.

However, New Lanark, the cotton-spinning village established by David Dale and Richard Arkwright, represents so much more than simply the industry which sparked it off and cannot be recommended too highly. Much the same can be said of the Summerlee Heritage Museum in the iron town of Coatbridge or the maritime museum in Irvine, both making valuable and highly individual contributions to knowledge and enjoyment.

Paisley is well-known for its thread making and textile associations but it is sometimes forgotten that Glasgow was a centre for the spinning and weaving of cotton, from the late 18th century up to about 1865, until the collapse of the Western Bank — in which several of the major firms had funds — and the cotton famine caused by the American Civil War contributed to the industry's downfall. Cotton had replaced tobacco as the city's major business interest and it, in turn, was superseded by heavy engi-

Schemes such as the landscaping of this once-derelict site of the North British Locomotive Company works in Springburn, are breathing new life into Glasgow

neering.

Glasgow is still a Victorian city and has many fine buildings; some, such as the Stock Exchange, having modern interiors behind a retained fascia. It is always possible to mourn examples of tragic losses but much of the output of prominent architects such as Alexander "Greek" Thompson and Charles Rennie Mackintosh can still be seen. In recent years many of the city's buildings — including humble tenements — have been stone-cleaned and restored to a glory most people had forgotten or never knew. Not so long ago, a privately-owned house being built in Glasgow was something of an event. Now people are once again living in the city centre and the transformation of the Merchant City is a credit to Glasgow. There have been the inevitable mutterings of "a yuppy takeover" but, as has been pointed out, in Glasgow the definition of a yuppy is someone with a job.

The new confidence being felt by the city is reflected in its tourist attractions, such as the renowned Burrell Collection, set amid parkland on the outskirts of the city. Like all the council-run museums, and each is special in its own way, entrance is free. Add to this the historic cathedral and the open spaces of the city's many parks, and the 1990 City of Culture Year slogan "There's a lot Glasgowing on" can be seen to be true.

It is also an ideal centre for getting around the West of Scotland, an area steeped in history and rich with leisure facilities such as the Magnum Centre in Irvine, the man-made Strathclyde Park or the fascinating Culzean Country Park. In less than an hour the train traveller can be on the bonnie banks of Loch Lomond or taking the sea breezes of the Firth of Clyde, where the steamer services give access to islands such as Cumbrae, Arran and Bute.

The trails in this book are only a rep-resentative sample of what can be done. None should present any problems of access but a word of warning may not go amiss. It is often said that there is no law of trespass in Scotland. This is not strictly true, although the law does differ from that which applies in England. It most certainly does not mean that the walker is free to wander at will and it is in everyone's interest that the tolerant attitudes of Scotland should continue. ❑

Railway history

THE origins of railways in Strathclyde lie with the need to move coal. Early in the 19th century, the Duke of Portland, seeking a means of transporting coal some ten miles from Kilmarnock to Troon Harbour, decided upon a wagonway — an

Plaque at Kilmarnock commemorating Scotland's first "proper" railway

early form of railway used in mines to carry coal from the pit to road, river or canal for onward transport. This "wagonway", however, was much closer to the concept of railways as we know them than any of its predecessors and marked a significant point in Scottish railway history.

Opened in 1812, it was the first line in the country to be sanctioned by Act of Parliament and the first to be carried on a viaduct over water; it utilised cast iron plate rails, laid double-track to a gauge of four feet, and it carried passengers — with horses pulling coal wagons from the Duke's pits during the week and trippers from Kilmarnock to the coast on Saturdays.

After some five years, a steam locomotive, the first in Scotland, was introduced. Built by George Stephenson and known as *The Duke*, it remained on the railway for 30 years and was represented in the coat of arms of the burgh of Troon. There is still a silver model of it in the town hall.

The Kilmarnock and Troon continued as a horse-operated wagonway until 1846, when it was leased to the Glasgow, Paisley, Kilmarnock and Ayr Railway and relaid for standard gauge locomotives. The viaduct over the River Irvine at Gatehead was bypassed in the upgrading, but is still in existence. It can be seen by train passengers on the Kilmarnock to Barassie line, which crosses the river on a newer bridge to the south. In April 1989 two commemorative plaques were unveiled; one at the procurator fiscal's office in Kilmarnock and the other at Troon marina, the nearest practicable sites to the original ends of the railway.

Returning to the 19th century, the next important event in Scottish railway history occurred in 1824, when the Monkland and Kirkintilloch Railway was granted its Act — the first specifically to authorise the use of locomotives. Landowners and coalmasters in the Airdrie area were behind this railway, the purpose of which was to take coal to the Forth and Clyde Canal at Kirkintilloch, for shipment westward to Glasgow — thus breaking the monopoly held by the Monkland Canal — and eastward to Grangemouth or by the Union Canal to Edinburgh.

The M & K began operations in 1826 but it was not until 1831 that the option to use locomotives was taken up, when two were obtained from Glasgow engineers Murdoch Aitken and Company. Thus began the city's long tradition of

Right: The 08.38 from Glasgow to Dunblane climbs the Cowlairs incline out of Glasgow's Queen Street station, August 1983

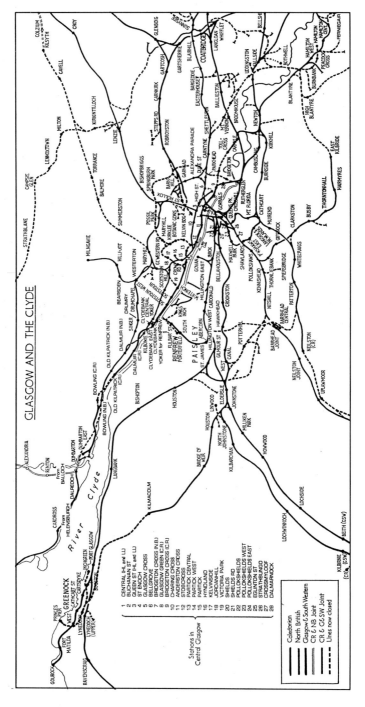

GLASGOW AND THE CLYDE

Stations in Central Glasgow

1 CENTRAL (HL and LL)
2 BUCHANAN ST
3 QUEEN ST (HL and LL)
4 ST ENOCH
5 GLASGOW CROSS
6 BELLGROVE
7 BRIDGETON CROSS (N.B.)
8 GLASGOW GREEN (C.R.)
9 BRIDGETON CROSS (I.C.R.)
10 CHARING CROSS
11 ANDERSTON CROSS
12 STOBCROSS
13 PARTICK CENTRAL
14 PARTICK WEST
15 PARTICK
16 HYNDLAND
17 KELVINSIDE
18 JORDANHILL
19 VICTORIA PARK
20 SHIELDS
21 SHIELDS RD
22 POLLOKSHIELDS
23 POLLOKSHIELDS WEST
24 POLLOKSHIELDS EAST
25 EGLINTON ST
26 STRATHBUNGO
27 CROSSMYLOOF
28 DALMARNOCK

Caledonian
North British
Glasgow & South Western
CR & NB Joint
CR & G&SW Joint
Lines now closed

The official opening of the Garnkirk and Glasgow railway, September 1831, with Tennant's chemical works dominating the background.

supplying locomotives to railways all over the world. From the outset, the M & K employed Birkinshaw patent iron rails on stone sleepers, which were better suited to locomotives than the iron tramplates of the Kilmarnock and Troon. It is fair to say the M & K *Number 1* was the first commercially successful steam locomotive in Scotland.

In the same month — May 1831 — that the first locomotive was delivered to the M & K, the third significant railway in Scotland was opened for goods traffic. This was the Garnkirk and Glasgow, promoted to provide an all-rail route for Monklands coal. It was actively supported by the Tennant brothers, whose Townhead chemical works lay at the western end of the line. The eastern extremity, eight miles away, was

Left: Map of railways in the Glasgow area in the mid-1970's indicating their original promoters

a junction at Gartsherrie with the M & K, with whom the Garnkirk and Glasgow was in direct competition. It is notable that the first name in its title was that of a relatively obscure Monklands hamlet, which indicates how the initial traffic flow was perceived by the promoters.

The Garnkirk set out to offer high-speed (by the standards of the time) conveyance of both passengers and goods, for which two locomotives of the latest design were ordered from George Stephenson. An elaborate and impressive ceremonial opening on September 27, 1831 demonstrated the capabilities of the steam locomotive. In day to day working, however, horses were also employed.

Haulage on the early railways was therefore a mixture of steam, horse and inclined plane (in which wagons descending an incline cable-hauled a corresponding rake up the slope). Important as these lines were, they were hardly trunk routes. This milestone was reached on July 15, 1837, when the Glasgow, Paisley, Kilmarnock and Ayr and the Glasgow, Paisley and Greenock railways were authorised. Construction of the Ayr route was brisk and the opening was in sections, beginning with Ayr to Irvine in August 1839 and culminating in Howwood to Beith exactly a year later. The Greenock line did not begin operations until March 1841, the cutting at Bishopton proving particularly time-consuming. The two railways shared a joint line between Glasgow and Paisley, which opened to traffic in July 1840, the city station being in Bridge Street, immediately south of the River Clyde. By the early 1840s, the foundations of a major section of the existing Strathclyde rail network were laid — albeit with rudimentary stations and lack of passenger comfort; third class travellers were conveyed in open trucks, without seats.

The obvious attractions of a railway linking Glasgow and Edinburgh, Scotland's two principal cities, resulted in this being the next major route to be opened. For $44\frac{1}{2}$ miles from Edinburgh to Cowlairs, the Edinburgh and Glasgow Railway swept along on an almost dead level course. A 36-arch viaduct, one-third of a mile long, spanned the Almond Valley with another similarly impressive structure over the River Avon near Linlithgow. Tunnels were required at Winchburgh and Falkirk and massive cuttings were blasted out of the rock at Philipstoun, Croy and Bishopbriggs: all to create a magnificently engineered high-speed line.

The gloss was somewhat taken off this feat of civil engineering excellence by the Forth and Clyde Canal Company's opposition to its Port Dundas branch being bridged by the E & G, as it dropped down the one and a quarter miles from Cowlairs to its proposed terminus in Queen Street. The railway

had to go under the canal, thus saddling itself and its successors with an operating liability in the form of a tunnel with a one-in-46 gradient, which necessitated a stationary engine and cable haulage of outgoing trains and special brake wagons for descending traffic. It was not until 1909 that it was felt that locomotives were sufficiently advanced for the incline to be worked by adhesion, although banking assistance (the addition of a second locomotive at the rear of the train) was the normal practice until well into the 1980s.

On New Year's Day 1842, the year the railway opened, the public were invited to view and presumably admire the whitewashed, gas-lit tunnel. They responded in droves; many had to be turned away. Such was the attraction of the new wonder of the railway age.

Meanwhile, moves were being made to establish a trunk line between Carlisle and Scotland. The respective merits of the Nithsdale (via Dumfries) and the Annandale (via Beattock) routes were hotly discussed and disputed. The decision, by what was to be termed the Caledonian Railway, to back the Annandale option brought to the fore again the railways of the Monklands, which had proliferated since the early 1830s. The Caledonian gained access to Glasgow by taking over the Wishaw and Coltness and the Glasgow, Garnkirk and Coatbridge, as it now was. This annexing of local lines gave rise to one of those anomalies which beset railway working and one which persisted until nationalisation in 1948. In order to link up with the Scottish Central Railway at Greenhill — and thereby gain access to points north — the Caledonian had to build a ten-mile branch from Gartsherrie. The first 52 chains or five-eighths of a mile of this were on Monkland and Kirkintilloch Railway metals. The M & K became part of the Monkland Railway Company which in turn was absorbed by the Edinburgh and Glasgow Railway and, in quick succession, the North British Railway. The Caledonian's main route to Perth and beyond was therefore dependent upon a rival's mineral line. This continued throughout the LMS and LNER eras.

The mid-1840s produced a short-lived period of railway mania. A significant scheme which did come to fruition was the Glasgow, Barrhead and Neilston Direct Railway of 1848, whose South Side terminus was located in the city's Pollokshaws Road, near the present Gushetfaulds freight terminal. The Caledonian, utilising the Pollok and Govan Railway, also made use of South Side.

The Caledonian found the Townhead terminus of the GG & C totally unsuitable, hence the opening in 1849 of Buchanan Street station. This was achieved by leaving the original route at what became Milton Junction and descending two miles — through the chemical waste dumps of Tennants factory and a tunnel under the Forth and Clyde Canal — to emerge north of Dobbies Loan, in the city. A relieving arch was required at the

tunnel mouth, to accommodate the Queen Street tunnel below. Buchanan Street station closed in 1966 and the site was subsequently redeveloped, with ScotRail House occupying part of it. In 1990, the only surviving reminder was the tunnel portal.

In the 1850s, the Glasgow Dumbarton and Helensburgh formed the basis of much future development, its completion in 1858 providing a continuous route along the north bank of the Clyde for the first time. The North British Railway took over the line 1865. The decade which followed saw an upsurge of expansionism, chiefly the City of Glasgow Union Railway, a massive undertaking which is worthy of close inspection, both for its impact on the growth of city rail services and the insight it provides on railway politics of the 1860s.

Bridging the Clyde

A special relationship, to use a 20th century term, existed between the Edinburgh and Glasgow Railway and the Glasgow and South Western Railway

Lanark-bound service on the main Glasgow to Carlisle route near the village of Cartland

(which had been formed by an amalgamation of the the Glasgow, Paisley, Kilmarnock and Ayr and the Glasgow, Dumfries and Carlisle). They were united against a common enemy, the Caledonian, and separated by the River Clyde. Exchange traffic between the two allies either had to take a very long detour or go by the hated Caledonian; hence the reason for the E & G and GSWR promoting a north-south link. Originally, a joint station was proposed on the north bank of the river, in which the Caledonian was to be included, as all of the city's termini were hopelessly inadequate. The Caley withdrew, to go its own way. In the great amalgamations of 1865, the North British Railway absorbed the E & G and became the northern partner.

The CGU left the NBR at Springburn, dropped by way of Alexandra Parade and Duke Street to Bellgrove then swung south-west to cross the Clyde at Hutchesontown before linking with the GSWR at Pollok Junction, near Shields Road. Much of it was in cuttings, through tunnels or on arches. It is hardly surprising that the six-mile line took 11 years to build and cost £2 million. A branch served the magnificent station and hotel at St Enoch Square; itself a major source of delay and expenditure. The station opened in 1876, as did the last section of the CGU. Apart from the St Enoch traffic, it was essentially a freight line, serving the NBR's new goods station at College, which was used by both railways, giving the GSWR access to the east of Scotland and the NBR access to the south-west and England.

Suburban passenger use was slow to develop but once it did, the line really came into its own. Spurs and branches turned the CGU into the core of a vast suburban network, linking the shipyards of the Clyde, Paisley's mills, locomotive building in Springburn and countless other engineering concerns with the city

centre and moving tens of thousands of workers around every day, many of them in the special workmen's trains which became a feature of Clydeside life.

In 1883 the GSWR took over the approaches to St Enoch and the station itself, establishing its headquarters there. Thirteen years later, the CGU was split between the partners, the NBR having the northern section to College Junction and the GSWR the rest, each retaining running powers over the other's domain. Today, the CGU is intact — apart from St Enoch and its associated lines — but only the section from Springburn to Bellgrove has a passenger service, as part of the Glasgow North electric system. The cross-river link is little used and has been rejected for incorporation in a north-south electric route, chiefly because of the need to construct a linking chord at the north end which would require relocating High Street station platforms, and the view that, as most journeys are to the city centre, more travellers would thereby be inconvenienced than would benefit. It is to be retained, however, as part of the strategy for a possible light railway network.

The Cathcart Circle

In 1861, the population of the district of Cathcart, south of Glasgow, was 3,000. Twenty years later, this had grown to 26,700, according to the prospectus for the Cathcart District Railway, issued in 1881. The district, claimed the promoters, possessed "every condition necessary for a pleasant and healthy place of residence". Except, presumably, a railway. The Cathcart District Railway was a local enterprise in the mould of some of the more rural lines. The Caledonian Railway had agreed to put up 50 per cent of the authorised share capital of £175,000; the rest was raised by local subscription, with some prospective passengers each purchasing one £10

Pollokshields East — the scene of a murder in 1945 and a major fire in 1976

Pollokshields West station, on the Cathcart Circle, awaits the resolution of a planning wrangle

share.

Even before the first sod was cut, the proposal for a circular route with a branch to Carmunnock was reduced to a line from Pollokshields East (as it became) to Cathcart. Construction proved painfully slow; the original contractors had to be replaced (but not without an acrimonious legal dispute) and it was not until May 1886 that the first train arrived at Cathcart. Construction, much of it involving high-walled cuttings and underpinning of buildings, had taken $3\frac{1}{2}$ years — more than twice the original estimate.

Despite the difficulties, the directors retained their entrepreneurial spirit and, with their railway carrying 100,000 passengers a month, were soon actively considering a westward extension to complete the circle. There would, of course, be fewer constructional problems as most of the route was through empty fields, which the CDR, with commendable courage, envisaged laid out as housing for season ticket-holding commuters. The line, as built, therefore crossed countryside on massive bridges, designed to accommodate roads which as yet did not exist. The three-mile extension, all of which was on either embankments or bridges or in cuttings, cost £140,000 or less than half the figure for the first $2\frac{1}{2}$ miles to Cathcart. On April 2, 1894, the Cathcart Circle, the line which became an institution, opened for business.

Confusion arose in the minds of passengers over the terms Inner and Outer Circle, resulting in some taking longer journeys than necessary. This could be compounded by the fact than the stations, of similar appearance, were poorly lit. It was not too difficult to become disorientated! (For the record, Inner Circle is via Maxwell Park and Outer Circle is via Queens Park.)

As the empty fields of the extension became the districts of Langside, Pol-

lokshaws, Shawlands and Maxwell Park, the stations developed into focal points of the area, the bookstall often being the only shop. By the turn of the century, there was a train every 10 minutes on the Circle and the fares were incredibly low; a return from Cathcart to the city, for instance, was cut to twopence halfpenny in 1902 to meet the challenge from the recently-electrified tramcars.

The Lanarkshire and Ayrshire Railway, from Newton to Cathcart and from Cathcart via Whitecraigs and Neilston to Ardrossan, was built to give the Caledonian an independent route for Lanarkshire coal being shipped from Ardrossan. By utilising part of the Cathcart Circle, a passenger route from Glasgow Central was also provided. The L & A has been truncated at Neilston but what remains is an integral part of the southern Glasgow suburban electric network, along with the Cathcart Circle.

The Cathcart District Railway, although firmly under the thumb of the Caledonian, remained nominally independent until the grouping of 1923. It was essentially a railway for people and parcels. The Glaswegian practice of going home for lunch admirably suited the Circle; it also came into its own when transporting tens of thousands of football fans to the big games at Hampden, a role it still fulfils.

Electricity did not reach the stations until 1958; otherwise the years have taken their toll. The signalboxes have gone, as have the decorative gardens. Stationmasters no longer live in the arches of the viaduct east of Shawlands station and many of the stations have been destaffed. Fire has been responsible for the replacement of some original buildings by new structures. Part of Pollokshields East went up in flames on April 21, 1976 and the subsequent demolition of the waiting room caused the demise of a particularly chequered part of the Circle's history — the mark of a bullet fired in the course of a robbery in 1945 which resulted in the deaths of two railway staff. Some ten months later, with no signs of an arrest forthcoming, a railway fireman walked up to a points policeman in Glasgow, handed him a Luger pistol and confessed to the crime. At his trial, it was revealed that his haul was a wage packet containing £4 3s 8d (£4.18).

The battle for the piers

The early railways from Glasgow to the Clyde Coast, chiefly the Glasgow Paisley and Greenock, were in direct competition with the river steamer operators and both sides indulged in near-suicidal fare-cutting. Once the masses had experienced sea breezes, the day tripper was born and the traffic figures boomed. This unfortunately was not reflected in the profit and loss account. The railway gained the upper hand, delivering passengers to the steamers at Greenock. This was taken a stage further in the mid-1860s when a line from Port Glasgow to Wemyss Bay offered a fast rail and ship route from Glasgow to Rothesay — for just half-a-crown ($12^{1}/_{2}$p) return. All of this was effectively controlled by the Caledonian Railway, a monopoly which was not to last.

The Greenock and Ayrshire Railway, as its title implies, was a local enterprise intended to boost Greenock as a seaport, by attracting minerals from Ayrshire. It involved a new pier at Greenock and was to be worked by the Glasgow and South Western Railway, with which it would be linked via the Bridge of Weir branch. In truth, no matter how it was packaged, the new railway was a major threat to the Caledonian-backed route.

The Caley's worst fears were soon realised and a fares war reminiscent of that of 25 years earlier ensued. The GSWR fledgling deposited its passengers close to the steamers at its newly-built Princes Pier, sparing them the trudge from station to pier required of GP & G ticket holders. Steamer operators tried to have the best of both worlds by calling at both Princes Pier and Custom House Quay but the public voted with their feet and patronised the Greenock and Ayrshire.

Sanity eventually prevailed and a joint purse agreement fixed realistic fares and timings, leaving the G & A ahead on points. The Caledonian turned its attention to its Wemyss Bay route and an uneasy peace descended.

One word shattered the calm: GOUROCK. The Caledonian had long had its eye on the place as a site for an ocean terminal for transatlantic liners. Its attempt at achieving this was defeated by the GSWR and the town of Greenock, both seeing their livelihoods threatened. However, the Caledonian was not to be put off — not even by the prospect of a very long tunnel. This, at one mile 344 yards, is the longest railway tunnel in Scotland, blasted out of the red sandstone between Greenock West station and Fort Matilda. The new pier was equally impressive, being bigger than its rival and nearer to the main resort of Dunoon. Its accompanying station was parallel to the steamer berths, allowing rapid transfer of passengers. All this and the Caledonian still had a card to play...

When the steamboat operators proved reluctant to commit themselves wholeheartedly to the new pier, the Caledonian's response was to form a subsidiary, with four vessels; the Caledonian Steam Packet Company. When the Wemyss Bay operator took umbrage at this, the CSPC replaced him and his boats with two brand new steamers.

The GSWR hit back by setting up its own steamer fleet and rebuilding Princes Pier and station. As the century neared its close, and that peculiarly Victorian phenomenon, the seaside resort, was in its heyday, the two sides were set for another fierce struggle. However, the contest was not two-sided but triangular and for the third contestant we have to look across the Clyde.

The amalgamations of 1865 gave the North British Railway a route from Glasgow to Helensburgh and Balloch. It began operating steamer services from Helensburgh in 1866 to Dunoon, Rothesay and Ardrishaig but these were abandoned after five months. The NB consolidated on the Dunoon, Holy Loch and Gareloch routes and, through its nominee the North British Steam Packet Company, became the first major railway company to operate a Firth of Clyde steamer fleet. In 1882 the activity on the south bank caused it to consider expansion. A major drawback was that Helensburgh pier was a ten-minute walk from the station and the good people of the town had the sense to resist all attempts to link the two by rail.

The answer was a new pier at Craigendoran, complete with station boasting through and bay platforms. It came into full use in 1883, with the North British entering the battle for the Rothesay traffic.

It was not just the holidaymaker and day tripper who provided the impetus for all this investment. The merchants of Glasgow had been encouraged to move house to the healthier air of the Firth of Clyde and considerable commuter business existed between the city and seaside hamlets such as Kilcreggan, Blairmore, Kilmun, Strone, Sandbank and Hunter's Quay, as well as large resorts such as Rothesay and Dunoon. Each railway's steamers picked up commuters from piers dotted throughout the Firth, whisking them to Gourock, Princes Pier or Craigendoran where fast trains awaited. There was very little to choose between each contestant's timings but the competition benefited the

passenger and kept fares down.

After the outbreak of the First World War, things were never quite the same. In the years that followed, the commuter traffic declined but the excursion business stood up well, until changing social patterns and the domination of the motor car altered the entire structure of Firth of Clyde cruising. Nationalisation brought rationalisation and Princes Pier was the first to lose its steamer services, although in the 1950s and 60s it served transatlantic liners (shades of the Caledonian's aspirations for Gourock in 1877). This ceased in 1965 and the site became a container terminal until 1987.

Craigendoran, weed-strewn and disused since 1972, is visible from the now-single-track electrified line to Helensburgh. Only Gourock has survived; the station refurbished in 1987 and the building shortened. Fast vessels still depart for Dunoon but now they are car ferries.

The story is similar at Wemyss Bay, terminal for Rothesay, except that the magnificent Caledonian Railway station of 1903 is largely intact, a tribute to combining functionality with aesthetic beauty. It was designed to handle crowds, hence its curved surfaces and wide passages.

It should be remembered that the Caley and the Sou' West were also in competition for the lucrative Arran traffic, each having its own station and pier in Ardrossan. With the same excessive duplication of resources that other parts of the Firth were witnessing, one company's steamer would follow its rival around the piers of the island, thus fragmenting such business as there was. (Those who observed the 1987 deregulation of bus services may see remarkable parallels in all this!) Not even the Victorians could put up with such nonsense and a traffic agreement was agreed upon.

Ardlui station, the northern limit of the Strathclyde PTE Day Tripper ticket, at the head of Loch Lomond

North bank developments

More than 100 years before the Scottish Exhibition Centre took shape near Finnieston in Glasgow, the same site was also the focus of major construction activity, as the 33-acre Queens Dock was built. Expensive to construct, the branch — on which the present stations of Anniesland, Hyndland and Partick now lie — took a wide sweep from the Helensburgh line at Maryhill, approaching Stobcross, as the dock was originally called, from the west. The yard was above the quays, the two being connected by a steeply dropping line. It was a North British enterprise, over which the Caledonian was granted running powers, although its traffic's progress was notoriously slow. The shipyards and engineering works of the industrialised north bank of the Clyde repre-

sented glittering prizes for any railway company, with the jewel in the crown being the town of Clydebank. Here were located the now legendary shipyard of John Brown's (served by the Glasgow Yoker and Clydebank Railway) and the vast Singer sewing machine factory, at one time the largest single industrial site in Scotland. The Caledonian Railway was none too pleased that its arch rival, the North British, had this lucrative area to itself.

Its assault began by backing the Lanarkshire and Dumbartonshire Railway, which received its Act in 1891. This paralleled the North British route, duplicating stations and wooing industrialists with low cost private sidings. It crossed the NB at Bowling, which became the location of two railways, a trunk road, the River Clyde and the Forth and Clyde Canal! Common sense prevailed over the proposal to have a separate Loch Lomond steamer fleet, pier and approach lines, and the Dumbarton and Balloch Joint line, in which the partners were the North British, Caledonian and Lanarkshire and Dumbartonshire railways, was the result. It controlled the Loch Lomond steamers and all the stations between Dumbarton East and Balloch, remaining a joint enterprise until nationalisation in 1948.

The present electrified route is an interesting historical mixture, being North British as far as Dunglass Junction, at the Bowling oil terminal. The NB line is truncated inside the terminal while the electrification follows the Lanarkshire and Dumbartonshire tracks to Dumbarton East, where the former junction with the NB has disappeared, and as far as Balloch is the old joint line. Meanwhile the Helensburgh and West Highland lines, which diverge from the joint line at Dalreoch, were pure North British. The existing route through Yoker is the old Glasgow Yoker and Clyde-

bank, which had been extended to Dalmuir.

The Lanarkshire and Dumbartonshire was denied access to the Singer plant for goods traffic but it played its part in transporting the army of workers required by Singer and its industrial neighbours. Clydebank had three railway lines and five stations and needed them all, as every day an operation of almost military proportions brought workmen in trains originating from such points as Airdrie, Bridgeton, Springburn and Balloch, until 1964 when the last train ran from Springburn to Singer. This mass movement was made possible only by bold and imaginative cross-city links.

Under the city streets

The underground railways of Glasgow play a vital role in the Strathclyde suburban network. Both Queen Street and Central have low level stations and there is, of course, the totally separate Underground or Subway circuit. The oldest

Above: The Airdrie-bound service leaves Balloch Central on the last day of its operation, April 23, 1988. The new station is on the left.

underground railway is the Queen Street line, which began life as the NBR-backed Glasgow City and District Railway of 1886. Only the fourth underground railway to be built in Britain, it linked the lines west of Stobcross with the City Union and the network to Coatbridge in the east.

The Caledonian's response, which was linked with the Lanarkshire and Dumbartonshire Railway already referred to, was to build its own east-west tunnel under the city centre. The Glasgow Central Railway struck westward from Dalmarnock to the projected L & D at Stobcross, from where it headed north to Maryhill, via Kirklee. By linking up various separate sections, a circular route of some 30 miles to Dalmarnock was created, running via Possil and Balornock, crossing the Glasgow-Edinburgh main line at what became Eastfield locomotive shed on the now-demolished Caley Brig.

The GCR was a massive undertaking, running as it did under the main city thoroughfares of Trongate and Argyle Street. Buildings had to be underpinned, including the Tron Steeple, which local opinion was convinced would come crashing down. Services such as sewers and gas and water pipes had to be diverted or relaid, the city benefiting at the railway's expense. Traffic had to be kept moving, but the horse-drawn tramcars were stopped at noon on Saturdays and work continued until 10pm the following day. Expertise of the highest order was required and the consulting engineer was John (later Sir John) Wolfe Barry, of London Underground fame; contractors were Formans and McCall, who built the West Highland Railway and the resident engineer was Donald Matheson, who was later to become General Manager of the Caledonian Railway. From Dalmarnock to Stobcross was only four miles but it took six years to build the GCR, which opened in August 1896. At last the Caledonian had a versatile passenger and freight network, much of which duplicated that of the North British. But there was ample business for both.

Terminal stations

To the Caledonian, one of the attractions of the new railway was that it would ease congestion at Glasgow Central which was now provided with a low level station. Before the opening of the Central in 1879, Glasgow lacked a decent terminus. Buchanan Street was seen as temporary, Queen Street was cramped, South Side was too far away and Bridge Street was inconvenient and inadequate.

The Caley's plans for a station at Dunlop Street were abandoned after the Admiralty insisted that the bridge over the River Clyde should be capable of opening. A station was subsequently established at Dunlop Street, but by the City Union Railway. In 1873, the Caledonian Railway (Gordon Street Glasgow Station) Act was passed, by which it appeared, the Caley would achieve its ambition of a north bank terminus. It allowed for the widening of an existing road bridge at Broomielaw, with a rail bridge on top, but it was found that too much valuable property would need to be demolished. A new Act was therefore obtained, to permit a deviation 50 yards downstream with a viaduct approach to a station between Gordon Street and Argyle Street. The layout at Bridge Street was altered to allow Caledonian trains to run to the new Central Station; meanwhile the GSWR insisted upon Bridge Street being enlarged.

When it opened, the Central was handling 134 trains a day. By 1887, this figure had increased to 300. Its eight platforms were narrow and short; there were no carriage sidings and no cab rank. A ninth platform was added in

1889 but it soon became obvious that a complete remodelling was the only answer. This time there were no half-measures. The platforms were doubled in length, aligned in serried ranks along a concourse whose area was increased by 20 per cent. The emphasis was on the speedy flow of passengers and to this end buildings were curved and corners rounded. The station was extended westward to permit construction of new platforms (numbers 10-13) and a 30 foot wide cab road accessed by tunnel from Hope Street. Expansion to the south was required to accommodate the longer platforms and a massive new bridge across the Clyde, carrying eight lines, which trebled the track capacity. It also covered over that part of Argyle Street between Union Street and Hope Street, creating what became known as the Heilanman's (or Highlandman's) Umbrella, under which Gaelic exiles from the highlands and islands would gather, each island or area favouring a particular shop window as its meeting place.

The reconstruction programme took place between 1901 and 1906 and by the time it was completed Glasgow Central (including the Low Level) was handling 22 million passengers a year, or an average of 600 trains per day. The station as it is today dates from then, although there have been recent additions, tastefully blending with the original. The torpedo-shaped building with its distinctive hand-positioned departure screens has been converted into shops and catering establishments. A new row of shops and restaurant on the former vehicle exit to Hope Street was opened in 1987, as was a new British Transport Police office. Both were built from scratch, although they blend in so well that this is difficult to believe. The same can be said of the Pullman Lounge in the north-east corner, whose curved windows skillfully match the original panelling alongside.

Down below, the Low Level system was closed in October 1964; travel patterns had changed and sulphurous

Glasgow Central interior dominated by the station's huge travel information indicator

Glasgow's Exhibition Centre station, formerly Finnieston, received this mural in 1988. It also welcomed many passengers thanks to its role as railhead for the National Garden Festival

caverns of stations and soot-encrusted trains encouraged no-one. (This was one reason why people deserted the railways for the newly-electrified tramcars at the turn of the century!) However, in 1979 the underground link was reborn as the Argyle Line, with new electric trains in the shape of Class 314 units, a new station — Argyle Street — plus reopened stations and a new burrowing junction with the north bank electrics near Stobcross, where the station was renamed Finnieston (later to become Exhibition Centre). As part of this scheme, a new interchange station was created at Partick, serving Central and Queen Street low level routes and a modernised Underground, of which more later.

While the Caledonian was addressing the problems of Glasgow Central, the North British had been active at Queen Street, which was enlarged between 1877 and 1888, the tunnel mouth being moved to the north side of Cathedral Street. Its crowning glory has to be the wrought iron arched roof, supported on cast iron Corinthian columns, the only one of its size and type to survive in Scotland.

The goods depot on the eastern side survived until the mid 1960s, when it made way for a car park and taxi ranks. Part of the exterior walls still stand. Essentially, the present station dates from 1968. Earlier, the Low Level station was rebuilt for the introduction of North Bank electrics in 1960, losing two platforms.

The other two main stations in the city have disappeared; St Enoch closing in June 1966 and Buchanan Street in November of the same year. St Enoch, a Victorian edifice which always seemed to reek of pigeon droppings, suffered the ignominy of acting as a car park until a shopping centre, opened in 1989, covered the site. Buchanan Street, at which little ever seemed to happen, is now ScotRail House and a college. ❑

Underground history

THERE is nothing new in traffic congestion. By the end of the last century, Glasgow city centre was frequently paralysed by the mass of horse-drawn vehicles which is why the Underground — or Subway as it was always known — was born. A six and a half mile circuit of twin tunnels, serving 15 stations, was built by the Glasgow District Subway Company. The route was under streets wherever possible, because the company's Act did not grant it wayleave rights, and buildings under which it wished to tunnel had to be purchased. The cut and cover method of construction was employed, with hydraulic shields used in soft or wet ground. Each tunnel was independent of the other and haulage was by continuous cable travelling at 12mph, which each train gripped or released as required. The drivers were in fact known as gripmen. Inside the Power House in Scotland Street, east of Shields Road station, eight boilers supplied steam to a pair of stationary engines which, by means of shafts and pulleys, drove the cables, which were kept under tension. The Power House had its own siding off the Glasgow and Paisley Joint Line, by which it received supplies of coal and cables.

One of the many peculiarities of the Glasgow system was that most stations were built on humps, the corresponding gradients assisting deceleration on approach and acceleration on leaving. Another oddity was — and still is — the

unique track gauge of four feet, shared by no other public transport undertaking in the world.

The original stations were St Enoch, Bridge Street, West Street, Shields Road, Kinning Park, Cessnock, Copland Road, Govan Cross, Merkland Street, Partick Cross, Hillhead, Kelvinbridge, St George's Cross, Cowcaddens and Buchanan Street. At street level, many of these had fairly anonymous entrances, located in tenement blocks. Buchanan Street was the deepest, the track being 40 feet below ground level. By contrast, at Kinning Park the distance was only 14 feet. Most stations were 156 feet long, with Cowcaddens longer and Hillhead and West Street shorter.

The public opening on December 14, 1896 followed three weeks of successful trial running, leaving the directors full of confidence about the new venture. The signalling was semi-automatic block with manually-controlled semaphores; trains could stop in their own length; stations were linked by telephone; and trains and stations were lit by electricity — in contrast to the gas lighting which prevailed above ground. What they failed to take into account was the enthusiasm of Glaswegians which resulted in vast crowds jamming the system by

Right: Copland Road station (now Ibrox) in 1935 showing a cable-hauled train on the Outer Circle and an electric train on the Inner

26

Bridge Street station in 1975, before the days of modernisation

8am on the opening morning. A cable fault caused a car to be dragged off the track near Buchanan Street, which restricted services to the Outer Circle, every car loaded to capacity. Late in the evening, car No 15 was rammed from behind by car No 5 and 17 people were injured. Services were suspended, not to resume until January 21, 1897.

Part of the problem on the first day had been that not all of the 30 cars ordered from the Oldbury Carriage and Wagon Company of Birmingham had arrived. The full complement was available for the reopening — all single-ended gripper cars — and these were soon supplemented by 24 four-wheel trailers from Hurst Nelson and Company of Motherwell. Further capacity was later obtained by splitting and lengthening the trailers (which were also placed on bogies) and purchasing more gripper cars from Oldbury.

Despite its relatively small circuit, the Subway in its early days served the main centres of commerce, many of the populated areas, and the shipyards and engineering works. As the city expanded, so too did competition from tramcars. A record 21 million passengers were carried in 1918 but the postwar trade depression, rising costs — particularly wages, coal and cables — and a damaging strike in 1920, put the company into the red. In 1922, after some negotiation, the Subway was taken over by Glasgow Corporation.

The new operators soon realised that electrification was inevitable and commissioned a report from consulting engineer WC Easton. The recommendations included third rail electrification, new signalling, new rolling stock, sweeping improvements to stations and construction of underground storage sidings. The total cost was estimated at £1 million and the Corporation's response was "thank you, but no thank you". Some 10 years later electrification was achieved — for £94,000!

The first step was the conversion of Car 60 in 1932, using Metropolitan Vickers 101DR tramway motors, giving a top speed of 30mph on a 1,985-yard electrified section of the Inner Circle between Merkland Street and Copland Road. The following year, the decision to electrify was taken, although not on the grand scale previously proposed, with the Tramways Department doing the work. Surviving cable-hauled stock was converted to either motor or trailer cars. All were given new Hurst Nelson bogies and motor cars also received new underframes from the same manufacturers. Heavier running lines were laid, with 80lb/yard replacing the original 60lb/yard, some of which was reused as conductor rail. Power was a 600-volt DC supply from the tramway system fed into the Subway at Shields Road, Partick Cross and Cowcaddens stations. The wooden stairways and platforms were replaced by concrete, in the interests of safety, and to mark the dawning of the electrified era, the Subway was officially rechristened Underground, although the name never really caught on with Glaswegians.

A full electric operation, on both circles, was achieved by December 1935, with the running time for the round trip cut from 39 to 28 minutes. An automatic signalling system based on London Transport practice had been installed in 1934, under which each train operated equipment which cleared a particular section to its rear. Trains carried portable telephones which could be clipped to wires on the tunnel wall in emergencies. The Power House, rendered redundant by electrification, was taken over by Howden Engineering in 1940, becoming a pattern shop and plate shop annexe.

The route mileage was 6.55 miles for the Inner and 6.57 miles for the Outer Circle and each train ran about 250 miles per day or 60,000 miles per year, at an average speed of 14mph. Cars were taken out of service for maintenance about every ten days, which involved yet another Subway peculiarity. There were no sidings or points on the system and the only access to the running circles was by means of a pit measuring 55 feet by 28 feet in the Broomloan Road car sheds, with vehicles lifted in or out by a travelling crane, the original of 12 tons capacity being replaced by one of $22^1/_2$ tons during electrification. Such was the degree of expertise, a defective car could be replaced within the three-minute headway between trains. Normally, following maintenance, a vehicle was returned to the opposite circle, in order to equalise wear. The hoist which was used acted as a turntable and transverser within the car sheds. Its massive hook broke twice — in 1957 and 1972. On both occasions, the victim was Car 32.

Until 1954, the livery was red and cream, lined out in black, with the "unseen" side painted dark red (contrary to the popularly-held belief that this side was not painted at all!) The livery then became all-red with a grey roof, the hidden side becoming the same shade as its counterpart from 1962. Inside, motor coaches had red leather upholstery; trailers had brown. The trailers in particular suffered from the ravages of time and in the late 1950s and early 1960s were taken to Coplawhill Tramway Works for body strengthening. As the 20th century wore on, the Subway became more and more a living museum. The staff called themselves The Moles, due to their subterranean existence. The drivers wore cap badges which read Corporation Tramways; inspectors displayed black braid on their uniform cuffs, a throwback to the days of national mourning for Queen Victoria. Some of the stations were renovated for the 1938 Empire Exhibition, held at Bellahouston Park, while others were tackled in the 1950s and 60s. The work included removing entrance canopies, installing new signs and repainting.

From 1958, power was purchased from the South of Scotland Electricity Board, to which Glasgow Corporation had sold Pinkston Power Station.

The Glasgow tramcars, which posed such a major threat to the Subway (and other suburban railways) 60 years earlier, disappeared from the streets in September 1962 — the last in Britain to go. Down below, the Subway soldiered on, kept going by displaced tram personnel and, more importantly, ex-tram motors. Spares for almost any piece of Subway equipment had long since become unavailable. Life-expired components were cannibalised for reusable parts but often the only option was to manufacture parts on a one-off basis. Quaint as this may be, it was no way to run a major transport undertaking. The individuality and isolation which was so much a part of the Subway's character was in danger of being the cause of its demise.

Various alternatives were put forward for the future of the network, ranging from modernisation to closure. The uncertainty surrounding it is illustrated by the fact that the Scottish Transport Group, when it was set up in 1969, was granted powers to operate a "subway". And there was only one "subway" in Scotland!

All this ended in 1973 with the creation of the Greater Glasgow Passenger Transport Executive which came up with a modernisation scheme costed at £12 million and eligible for a 75 per cent Government grant. By this time passenger journeys had dropped from a 1949 peak of 37.3 million to 13 million a year due to population shifts, industrial decline and rising fares.

The Clockwork Orange

The scale of the PTE modernisation project was such that the Underground would have to close completely. In the event, this happened prematurely, on

Partick rail and underground exchange station

May 21, 1977, due to damage caused by work already under way. Perhaps the greatest upheaval was at St Enoch, where the ornate station building, which was once also the headquarters of the Subway Company, required to be underpinned while a new station was constructed below. A new Underground access was provided and the building has been retained as a travel centre. Merkland Street station was incorporated into a new British Rail interchange station called Partick, which is also served by bus routes. (This replaced Partickhill BR station.) Govan Cross, which became simply Govan, has been totally rebuilt, as has the surrounding area, and is also integrated with bus services. Partick Cross was renamed Kelvinhall (the station signs portray the name as one word) and Copland Road became Ibrox, the changes reflecting the areas actually served.

Many Underground station buildings now have distinctive street level buildings which stand out among their surroundings, in contrast to their self-effacing predecessors, due in part to the open spaces created by mass demolition of the city tenements. At Kelvinbridge, the original entrance can still be seen, opposite the present building. An escalator links it with Great Western Road; escalators have also been installed at St Enoch, Partick, Govan Cross, Shields Road, Hillhead, St George's Cross and Cowcaddens. Buchanan Street has an escalator to street level plus moving ramps between the Underground and Queen Street ScotRail station. Nine of the 15 stations have island platforms, with the busier locations having two platforms.

The peculiar four-foot gauge was retained, with welded track laid on a concrete base. Points have also been installed, giving access to and from the surface-level car sheds, dispensing with the lifting pit. The Broomloan Road depot, as well as housing maintenance facilities, is also the nerve centre at which the controller can plot the position of every train, plus the aspect of each signal. Television cameras monitor each station platform, relaying to screens in the booking offices or to central control. Train operation is automatic, controlled by coded signals received from trackside transponders, with the drivers operating the doors and start signals and being generally responsible for passenger safety. Trains can be manually driven at the depot and in emergencies. Radio links drivers with each other and control and the clip-on telephone and tunnel-side wires provide another emergency contact.

The order for 33 new double-ended motorised cars was won by Metro Cammell of Birmingham, which incorporated the Oldbury Carriage and Wagon Company, builders of the original vehicles. A mock-up car went on display at the Scottish Design Centre in Glasgow in 1975, leading to the adoption of orange livery with a white stripe, since replaced by Strathclyde Red (which is nearer orange!) with black window surrounds and no white stripe. Doing the rounds at the time was the film *The Clockwork Orange*, which led to the system's nickname.

A flat-fare system, with automatic ticket barriers, was introduced, as was a ban on smoking, well ahead of a similar move in 1989 covering the Strathclyde rail network, imposed following the Kings Cross fire disaster.

Officially, the new Underground was inaugurated by the Queen — who travelled in Car 132 — on November 1, 1979, as was the £35 million Argyle Line, crossing the centre of Glasgow from Rutherglen to Kelvinhaugh. While the Argyle Line opened for revenue earning service on November 5, the public reopening of the Underground was not until April 16, 1980, due to delays in bringing the power and signalling systems into service and difficulties in overcoming flooding, which affected the automatic train-operation system. By then, the projected cost of £12 million had risen to £53 million.

A flat fare of 20p was charged, calculated on passenger journeys of 15 million annually; in the event only 9.9 million were recorded in the first full year. This had grown to under 14 million by the end of the 1980s. In recent times, the Underground has operated a frequency ranging from four minutes in the peaks to eight minutes in the evenings and on Sundays. The peak hour frequency could be doubled, but only with modifications to the signalling system. Each two-car train seats 76 passengers, with a further 104 standing. In late 1989, the purchase was announced of eight trailer cars, to enable all trains to operate with three vehicles. Park and Ride is a feature of several stations, with one ticket covering parking and travel. One of these, Kelvinbridge, was the scene of a mid-60s Park and Ride arrangement, utilising the former BR goods yard. West Street, always a quiet station, now has a 60-vehicle car park alongside. Bridge Street, which for a time was an island in a sea of demolition sites, is now surrounded by commuters' cars.

Over the years, extensions to the network have been considered and rejected. The same is true since Strathclyde PTE took over, with reviews and consultation documents generally agreeing that the high cost and upheaval would not be reflected in increased passenger usage. A Strathclyde Transport development study published in early 1990 concluded that no Underground extension option warranted further consideration.

One of the casualties of modernisation was the distinctive subway smell, which lingers in the minds of many people, if nowhere else. Until relatively recently, the view persisted among Glaswegian grannies that the Subway atmosphere was beneficial to sufferers of chest and breathing complaints. The original Subway system, with its creosoted wooden platforms and stairways and pitch-covered cables, obviously had an even more distinctive air, for it was thought to be a cure for whooping cough. Afflicted Glaswegian children were also encouraged to follow tar boilers, for which similar properties were claimed. There is little medical support for this old wives' tale, other than perhaps that a change of air does no harm.

It is certainly true that for many years, West Street had an aroma all of its own — but this was due to the fishmonger's shop next door! ❑

Strathclyde PTE

The new class 320 EMU

STRATHCLYDE Passenger Transport Executive grew out of the Greater Glasgow PTE, formed in 1973. When Strathclyde Regional Council assumed its responsibilities in 1975, the PTE became the Council's agent for the part of Strathclyde lying outside the PTE's designated area.

The sheer size and complexity of the Region meant that the PTE assumed responsibility for a wide variety of transport, from minor ferries to rural buses; from commuter rail services to the Glasgow Underground. The situation regarding buses changed with deregulation in October 1986 but the PTE local rail network is the largest outside London, with some 160 stations used by 38 million passengers annually. Another 15 stations on the Glasgow Underground are used by approaching 14 million passengers each year.

Over 48 per cent of all journeys to and from work in the Glasgow area are made by public transport and of these 24 per cent are made by rail (including the Underground). These proportions are higher than for any conurbation outside London. In 1988-89 the Section 20 grant (i.e the amount paid by Strathclyde Region to British Rail for providing services as decreed by the Council) was £26.71 million.

Strathclyde has traditionally been pro-rail, demonstrated by the reopening of the Argyle Line and the Paisley Canal route, the Ayrshire electrification and the considerable number of new, reopened or refurbished stations provided in recent years. The Region has also invested in new rolling stock, more recently in the form of Class 156 Sprinter sets and Class 320 Electric Multiple Units. Many of the innovations have been partly funded by grants from such sources as the Scottish Office or the European Community; however, first Strathclyde had to provide the impetus.

The Region's faith in rail has been strengthened by the substantial savings which have been made by such moves as destaffing stations, the deployment of "revenue protection" staff, and the implementation of the Strathclyde Manning Agreement which allows for driver-only operation of trains.

The way ahead?

A consultation document produced by the PTE in 1989 and entitled *Public Transport for the 21st Century* raised the options of either reducing the rail network or merely maintaining the status quo by replacing worn-out parts of the system on a like-for-like basis. It rejected both on the grounds that they would lead to increased car and bus trips. The document said: "It is not feasible to provide sufficient new roads to avoid chronic congestion, as has been demonstrated in urban centres throughout the world. It is quite clear therefore that if the quality of existing public transport levels is to be maintained serious consideration has to be given to enhancing provision."

The emphasis, therefore, had to be on expanding rail provision. The report rejected extension of the Glasgow Underground on several counts, although it made the point that in 1989 eight new trailer coaches were ordered, enabling all trains to be made up of three cars. On the rail network, it said there were two particularly attractive possibilities for reinstatement. These were the Northern Suburban Line and the Rutherglen-Coatbridge Line.

The Northern Suburban Line

The north Glasgow suburbs of Ruchill, Possil, Cadder, Summerston and Maryhill have no rail services. By building new stations on the existing rail line and introducing a Sprinter service between Queen Street High Level and An-niesland, it would be possible to provide a connection to both the city centre and to the rest of the bus and rail network at Anniesland. Some reinstatement of track would be needed between the former Knightswood South and Maryhill Park Junctions.

The cost of this option was put at £5 million, in the consultation document.

The Rutherglen-Coatbridge Line

In a similar fashion to the Northern Suburban Line concept, a number of communities, including Carmyle, Mount Vernon, South Baillieston, Bargeddie and South Coatbridge could be provided with a rail service by introducing Sprinters onto an existing freight route, operating from Coatbridge Central to Glasgow Central High Level. The line runs through Cambuslang Investment Park, which provides scope for an additional station (possibly privately-funded). This option has been costed at £7.5 million.

Other suburban rail developments

The possibility of reintroducing rail services to Larkhall was also referred to in the Consultation Document. This option would involve reinstating and electrifying a spur from the Hamilton Circle line between Hamilton Central and Motherwell. The attractiveness of this option has been enhanced by the possibility of significant residential development in the Larkhall area adjacent to the line.

The possibility of providing additional cross-city rail services in Glasgow by introducing passenger trains on the Tron freight line and building a new spur at High Street has been referred to earlier in this book *(see page 16)*. This opportunity was reconsidered in the 1989 Report, having been rejected in the 1987 Rail Review. However, despite strong support for the idea from certain groups, it was concluded by the PTE that the disbenefits for passengers bound for the city centre — in terms of longer journey times — would outweigh any benefits to cross-city passengers. Nevertheless, the 1989 document stated: "The Strathbungo Link, Tron Line and St Enoch Bridge represent major dormant assets which could be utilised to considerable effect in providing a mass rapid transit route from the city centre to the south side of the conurbation." In other words, as part of a Metro or Light Railway system.

Metro system?

The Development Study described proposals for a Southern and a Northern Metro, operating on existing rail routes, disused lines and on-street. On the south side of the city centre, the present lines to Neilston and Newton and the Cathcart Circle could form the core of a Metro system, with on-street extensions into, say, Castlemilk, Pollok and Newton Mearns, plus an on-street loop around the centre of the city

In the north, the core could be provided by the Drumgelloch and Springburn lines in the north and east and the Dalmuir via Singer and Milngavie routes in the west. Street-running suburban branches could be built in Drumchapel, Milngavie, Easterhouse, Balornock and Airdrie.

In the city centre, Metro trains could use the Queen Street low-level tunnel but continuation westward would involve major reconstruction work in the vicinity of Partick Interchange.

The northern and southern Metros could be connected by the Tron Line as it is believed that constructing the aforementioned St John's Link to Light Railway standards would not require property demolition.

The Northern Metro would require all main line trains from Helensburgh and Balloch to operate via Yoker and the Argyle Line, as would all West Highland Line trains. There would be reduced utilisation of the carriage cleaning and signalling centre at Yoker, but this would have to be set against enhanced frequencies on the Argyle and Queen Street Low Level lines by overcoming the existing bottleneck between Partick and Hyndland.

However, the preferred approach in the north would be to add a number of branches to the city centre loop created by the Southern Metro. These would, wherever possible, make use of segregated alignments such as central reservations, priority lanes and disused rail lines. This option, the partially-segregated strategy, was preferred by the vast majority of respondents to the Consultative Document.

Vehicles used by a Metro system would most likely be modern articulated trams, with a top speed of around 50mph. The study concluded: "By proper design, the street-running LRT would have no greater impact on general traffic conditions than conventional buses with no detriment regarding access to adjoining properties." ❑

RAIL NETWORK

Strathclyde Transport

⇌ 🇺 Travelator Link
Buchanan St 🇺 – Queen St ⇌

Interchange with Caledonian MacBrayne

Prestwick Airport

Glasgow Airport

Bus:
Prestwick Station – Airport Terminal

Bus:
Central Station
(Argyle Street – North Entrance)
Queen Street Station
(North Hanover Street)
Anderston and Buchanan Bus Station

Inter-terminal Bus Link

Park and Ride (Free Parking)

Ⓟ Parking Available

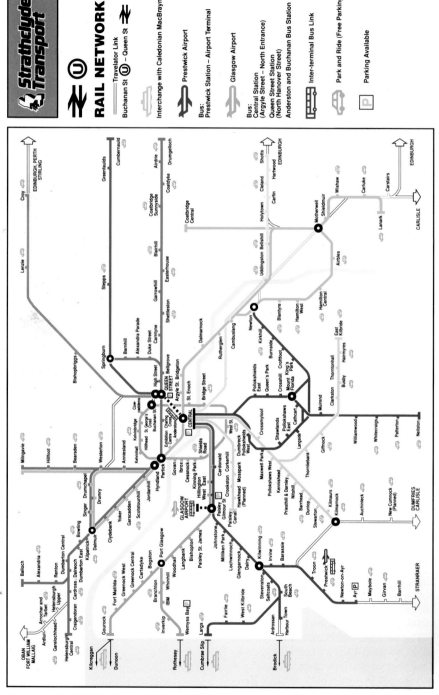

Glasgow trails

Pollok House — see museum and gallery trail

The following trails include an exploration of the work of one of Britain's greatest architects — Charles Rennie Mackintosh — as well as highlighting the city's historic importance as one of the world's greatest engineering centres and its 1990 status as the European capital of culture.

The east city

*Covers many heritage sights to be
seen east and north-east of the city
centre. (Around two miles)*

The famous Barras market

BEGIN at Bridgeton station, on the Argyle Line, and cross the pedestrian precinct to James Street, diagonally opposite. Walk along James Street, turn right at the traffic lights into Greenhead Street then bear left alongside Glasgow Green. The Templeton Business Centre looms up on the right but it is not until the far end of the building is reached that the real gem is revealed. Known, for obvious reasons, as the Doge's Palace, this stunning exercise in multi-coloured brickwork is architect William Leiper's response to the firm's desire to "erect instead of the ordinary and common factory something of permanent architectural interest and beauty". It is certainly of permanent architectural interest; the definition of beauty rests with

Right: Statue of David Livingstone with Glasgow Cathedral in the background

38

Top: Templeton's carpet factory — an attempt by architect William Leiper "to erect instead of the ordinary and common factory something of permanent architectural interest and beauty"
Left: Interior of the People's Palace winter gardens. The glazed roof is said to represent the inverted hull of Nelson's flagship, HMS Victory.
***Above:** People's Palace exterior*

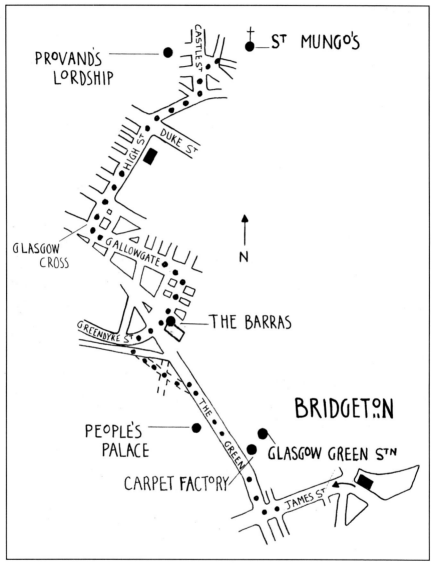

the individual.

It was built for the manufacture of spool Axminster carpets and was almost complete when, in November 1889, a partial collapse killed 29 women in an adjacent weaving shed.

Nearby is the former Glasgow Green station building, closed in 1953, which at first sight appears substantially intact but in fact consists of only two walls, below which electric trains on the Argyle Line rumble past. On Glasgow Green, in front of the Templeton factory, are the iron poles from which housewives traditionally hung their washing.

Until the middle of the 19th century, Glasgow Green was the only public recreation area in the city and was the scene of mass gatherings of every description, from Bonnie Prince Charlie's army to executions and political meetings. A great Liberal demonstration held in 1832 was attended by 70,000 people. James Watt is alleged to have been strolling across the Green in 1765 when he first thought of his condenser development of the steam engine, which was at the heart of the industrial revolution. It is ironic, therefore, that almost 100 years later the city fathers wished to mine the reserves of coal under the Green and were dissuaded only by the public outcry. A stone marking this link with Watt is located near Nelson's Column, erected in 1807, before the one in London's Trafalgar Square. The Green is also the location of the Doulton Fountain, put up for the Great Exhibition of 1888 and now sadly derelict. In more recent times, a proposal to build a motorway across part of the Green met with as much opposition as the coal-mining scheme.

About 100 yards from the Templeton factory is the People's Palace, a delightful museum crammed with items of local and national interest, from comedian Billy Connolly's banana boots to what is claimed to be the real Stone of Destiny (the English were allegedly fobbed off with a copy in the 1950s, after Scottish nationalists removed it from Westminster Abbey). It is worth allocating some time to tour the displays.

Major alterations at the rear of the building provided a lift, stairs and toilet facilities facing into the winter gardens, the glazed roof of which is said to represent the inverted hull of Nelson's flagship HMS Victory (complementing the Nelson memorial in Glasgow Green). The interior was re-landscaped in 1977 and is a pleasant place in which to linger over a cup of tea.

From the People's Palace continue to a large arch (which appears to be off-perpendicular) and right along Greendyke Street to London Road, where a gateway at Kent Street proclaims this is the entrance to the Barras, Glasgow's famous market, which on Saturdays and Sundays fills the surrounding streets with traders and customers. At the other end of Kent Street turn left into Gallowgate, noting on the far side of the road the Saracens Head pub, a hostelry which Dorothy Wordsworth described in 1803 as "quiet and tolerably cheap", and continue to Glasgow Cross, passing under the City Union Railway.

At the Cross, the flat open space in front of the Tolbooth steeple marks the location of the former Glasgow Cross station, on the Central low level route. Turn right up High Street — where the former huge Bell Street railway warehouse has been turned into flats — till High Street station, giving access to the suburban network, is reached. Behind is the site of the former College goods station and before that, of Glasgow University. A plaque on a wall nearby records this fact.

Either head for the trains or continue along High Street, with its ornate tenements on either side north of the Duke Street junction, and then, visible on the left, modern student accommodation heated by daylight energy, hence the unusual roofs. The area around the cathedral has recently undergone remodelling and new building, including a particularly fine example of modern techniques in a traditional style, to create a visitor centre. The lighting in the pedestrian precinct which has been created in front of the cathedral is decorated with the tree, fish, ring and bell associated with the city's coat of arms.

The cathedral is where the city began. It was founded in 1136 on the site of St Mungo's church of 543 AD and for centuries was at the heart of Christianity in Scotland, when Glasgow was essentially an ecclesiastic and (later) university settlement, bridging the Clyde.

The 1136 building was destroyed by fire and a replacement consecrated in 1197. The present church spans a construction period extending from the 13th to the 15th century yet is remarkably consistent in style; refreshingly outstanding in what is essentially a Victorian city. Important features include the lower church, which has been described as "a forest of stone pillars presenting a mystery of light and shadow". Here lies the tomb of St Mungo, who died in 603 AD. St Kentigern and St Mungo were one and the same, the name Kentigern meaning Chief Lord. He was commonly known as Mungo — or Dear One. The nearby St Kentigern's Tapestry is a modern work, dating from the late 1970s, and is the result of a bequest to the cathedral, specifically to enhance this part of the building. A push-button switch on the right-hand side illuminates the work.

The cathedral also has an important collection of post-war stained glass windows, the earliest of which, in the north wall, is the only example in the cathedral of the work of Douglas Strachan. The great east window, installed in 1951 and replacing one given by Queen Victoria, is by Francis Spear and shows the four evangelists, St Matthew, St Luke, St Mark and St John. The building survived the ravages of the Reformation relatively unscathed and is still in use as a church, although owned by the Crown.

Across Castle Street is the city's oldest house — Provand's Lordship, dating from the 15th century. Built as St Nicholas Hospital, it has been a manse, a public house and a sweet shop, among other things, with various structural alterations over the centuries. It is now a museum of aspects of the city's history and life, including displays of pottery and clay pipes whose manufacture was once an important industry in the surrounding area.

Return via the previous route to High Street station. ❑

The two-walled remains of Glasgow Green station — closed in 1953

Underground trail

Strathclyde PTE has produced an Underground heritage trail leaflet, available (at the time of writing) along with a day ticket allowing unlimited travel. Using some of the ideas in the leaflet, the following walks provide a number of suggestions for using the system to see several attractions in Glasgow, although exactly what is attempted in one day is best left to the individual.

Partick underground station

START at St Enoch Underground where the original and distinctive station building is now a travel centre. It was the work of architect James Miller, who was responsible for many railway stations and major hotels. The castle-like structure has survived the upheaval associated with modernising the Underground and has witnessed the demolition of St Enoch station, the Glasgow and South Western terminus of 1876, with its large hotel added three years later. The site is now a huge shopping centre, resembling a circus marquee made of glass. The station closed in 1966 but the hotel survived until 1974. During demolition, much of the rubble was tipped into Queens Dock which was being filled in in preparation for the construction of the Scottish Exhibition and Conference Centre.

James Miller was also the architect of the surviving reminder of Bridge Street station, the buildings of the 1890 extension, passed every day by countless trains in and out of Glasgow Central,

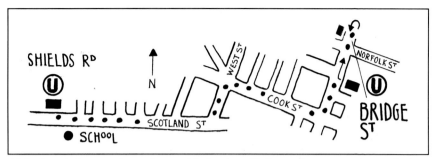

with electric locomotives often stabled in front of it. To view it from street level, alight at Bridge Street Underground, turn right and cross Norfolk Street and the former station is at numbers 40-52 Bridge Street, with a lion rampant plaque above the north door and the date 1890 above the south. With the opening of the greatly-enlarged Glasgow Central early this century, the Bridge Street extension became shops and offices.

Walk southwards along Bridge Street into Eglinton Street, turning right into Cook Street. Note the building with the tower at the Tradeston Street corner; it is a 1900 extension to an earlier paint warehouse. Turn left into West Street. Near the Underground station, a reminder of the London Midland and Scottish Railway is found on some of the iron pillars supporting a bridge, which display the letters LMS. Cross into Scotland Street, passing the site of the Subway power house on the left, in the

Lion and unicorn staircase at Glasgow University

premises of an engineering company, and Scotland Street School (see the Charles Rennie Mackintosh trail). Regain the Underground network at Shields Road station.

Heading clockwise around the circuit, it's worth alighting at Cessnock to view Walmer Crescent, round the corner from the station. This is the work of architect Alexander Greek Thomson — a little austere and regimented perhaps but nevertheless impressive, although the row of shops between it and Paisley Road West does nothing to enhance it.

Govan

Govan Underground station is surrounded by redevelopment; this being another of those Glasgow districts in which traditional buildings, open spaces and modern houses nestle somewhat uncomfortably. Rebuilding and industrial contraction have left their marks on the area and on the people, in a manner similar to, say, Springburn. Govan has always considered itself an area apart. When it was absorbed into Glasgow in 1912 (with Pollokshaws and Partick) it was the fifth-largest burgh in Scotland and had grown from being a fishing village to a major shipbuilding and engineering centre.

Two names dominated the district; Elder and Pearce. John Elder, partner in Randolph, Elder and Co, was at the centre of the development of the first successful compound steam engine for the marine market, which was, in its way, almost as significant as Watt's steam condenser. The firm moved into shipbuilding and established a yard at Fair-

field Farm, Govan, adding another name to Clyde history.

John Elder's untimely death at the age of 45 robbed the Clyde of a great engineer; it also resulted in control of the shipyard passing to the distinguished naval architect, William Pearce. When he died in 1888, he had been knighted, served as MP for Govan and left plans for a liner to cross the Atlantic in five days!

His statue stands opposite the Pearce Institute in Govan Road, gifted by the family in 1903 for the religious, educational, social and moral welfare of the people of Govan. It was designed by Sir Rowand Anderson, who was also responsible, in 1884, for the rebuilt Govan Old Parish Church and Glasgow Central station hotel. The church, next to the Institute, is an ancient ecclesiastical site and has a collection of Celtic headstones and monuments. *Access can be arranged by telephoning the church office on (041) 445 1941.*

Continue along Govan Road, past the former Fairfields yard (now operated by Kvaerner) which in the mid-1960s was the scene of the so-called Fairfields Experiment, in which the yard was owned by the Government, industry and trade unions and radical changes were made in working practices. It later passed to Govan Shipbuilders Ltd. Note

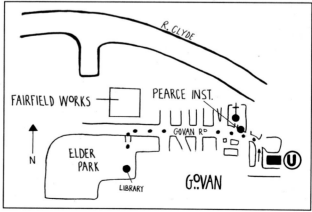

The Tenement House,
145 Buccleuch Street —
Left: kitchen
Below: parlour
Bottom: exterior

the carving adorning the office entrance. Cross into Elder Park, which contains a statue of John Elder, the library his widow gifted to Govan and also a memorial to the six Fairfield employees and 26 naval personnel who perished in the submarine K13 disaster in the Gareloch in 1917. There is a fascinating link here — the world's first chair of naval architecture, named after John Elder, was created at Glasgow University in 1883. One of the holders of the chair, Professor Percy Hillhouse, was a survivor of the K13 accident. Return to Govan Underground station by the same route.

University and museums

Take the Underground to Hillhead, turn left into Byres Road and left up University Avenue, with the tall tower of the Boyd Orr science building on the left, and enter the university grounds by the main gate on the other side of the road, at the top of the hill. Visitors are free to wander around the campus and excellent guide books are available from the visitor centre. Guided tours are also conducted on a limited basis. *Telephone (041) 330 5511 for details.*

If time is limited, see the Gothic tower, the view of the city from the flagpole vista point in front of the tower (becoming difficult in summer due to the height of the trees), the undercroft and the Bute Hall. Professors' Square has the lion and unicorn staircase from the Old College buildings in High Street and a Victorian pillar box, still in use. The Hunterian Museum is named after anatomist and physician, William Hunter (1718-1783) who bequeathed his collection of coins, minerals, paintings and books, now valued at well in excess of £100 million. It was Scotland's first public museum and exhibits include a fossilised shark from the Glasgow suburb of Bearsden and a dinosaur footprint from Skye. (The separate Hunterian Art Gallery across University Avenue should also be seen. As well as the Mackintosh house reconstruction, its collection of works by Whistler is outstanding.)

Leave the university by the Pearce Lodge gate in the north-east corner. This was a gift of shipbuilder Sir William Pearce (of Govan

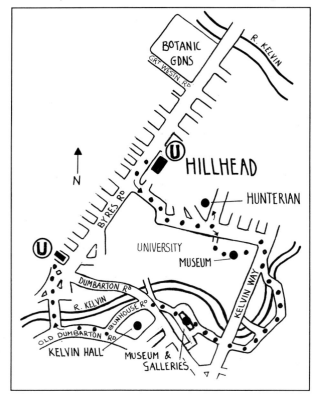

Converted mill with museums in background

Kelvingrove art gallery

fame) and incorporates the Old College gateway, surmounted by the royal arms of King Charles II, his initials CR2 and the Latin inscription recording the date of the original building as 1656. Turn right into University Avenue and right into tree-lined Kelvin Way. It contains an oak planted in 1918 to mark the attainment of votes for women.

Cutting through Kelvingrove Park, Kelvin Way has a speed limit of 20mph; however it is advisable to treat it like any other road as drivers certainly do! It is worth wandering off into the park on the left, if only to see one of the few working fountains to be found anywhere these days. The Stewart Memorial Fountain, commemorating the opening of Glasgow's Loch Katrine water supply system in the 1850s (thereby ridding the city of cholera and typhus), features sculptures on the theme of Sir Walter Scott's *Lady of the Lake*. It cost £2000 to build in 1872; restoring it to working order in 1988 cost £158,000.

Find your way back to Kelvin Way, in order to enter the part of the park containing the Art Galleries. The gate is near the four statues, representing progress and prosperity, navigation and shipping, peace and war and commerce and industry. One was restored under the supervision of the sculptor Benno Schotz after being damaged by enemy action on one of the nights of the infamous Clydebank blitz, in March 1941. It carries a plaque to that effect. Kelvingrove Park, opened in 1853, was planned by Sir Joseph Paxton, architect of London's Crystal Palace. It was the scene, in 1901, of an exhibition of art, industry and science, which covered 73 acres around the park. The machinery hall was on the site now occupied by the Kelvin Hall; a sports stadium was located in the university grounds where the chemistry department now stands. Opened on the same day as the exhibition were the new Art Galleries, partly financed by the

£54,000 surplus from the 1888 international exhibition.

The Art Galleries were designed to face the River Kelvin but the story grew up that they had been built the wrong way round and the architect committed suicide. The rumours were fanned no doubt by the main access becoming the one from Dumbarton Road. Like many good stories, it's untrue. As a building, it has been criticised, the fussy roofline in particular drawing adverse comment.

A reminder of the 1901 exhibition can be seen from the west end of the galleries, through the trees on the other side of the River Kelvin: the Port Sunlight cottages representing the last word in workers' housing, as found at Lever Brothers' industrial complex in Cheshire. (They must have come as a shock to the average West of Scotland working class family.) The cottages were presented to the city corporation after the exhibition and are still occupied. A total of 11.5 million people visited the 1901 exhibition, many of them travelling by the newly-electrified tramcar network.

Enter by the rear door — or is it the front? — and you are in the home of one of the finest civic art collections in Britain, including masterpieces such as Salvador Dali's *Christ of St John of the Cross* and Rembrandt's *A Man in Armour*. The collection, renowned in the art world, is arranged thematically. The building also has significant sections on armoury, Scottish and Egyptian archaeology, geology, and natural history, plus the Charles Rennie Mackintosh display referred to in the Mackintosh trail. With so much to see, allow plenty of time. The galleries attracted more than one million visitors in 1989, with the Transport Museum and the Burrell Collection coming next in the league.

Across Dumbarton Road is the Kelvin Hall, now a sports arena and home of the Museum of Transport, which was previously housed in the former Coplawhill tramcar works. Enter the transport museum by Bunhouse Road, alongside the River Kelvin. On the opposite bank, note the red sandstone building on Dumbarton Road — a sewage pumping station.

As with the Art Galleries, give yourself plenty of time to look around the Museum of Transport. Its exhibits include railway locomotives representing each of the five main Scottish companies, buses and tramcars, ship models, motor vehicles — some of historical significance to Scotland — and a fascinating recreation of a typical 1930s street, plus of course the Subway gallery with its full-size relics.

On leaving, turn left into Bunhouse Road and right into Old Dumbarton Road, where Bishop Mill has been converted to flats. Note the wheatsheaves on the top of each gable. Originally water-powered, the mill was electrified by the end of its working life. On its weir was built a bridge to carry the Lanarkshire and Dumbartonshire Railway across the Kelvin. Around the corner in Benalder Street is another L & D relic; the street-level booking office of Partick Central (or Kelvin Hall) station, which closed in 1965. Continue along Benalder Street to Dumbarton Road, on the other side of which is Kelvinhall Underground, by which you can return to your starting point. The total walking distance is around two miles but, in view of the time required at the two museums, it may be wise to treat them separately.

As an alternative to taking the Underground, walk the mile or so up Byres Road to the Botanic Gardens, at the corner of Great Western Road and Queen Margaret Drive. The park is full of exotic plants from all over the world, including those in Kibble Palace, a huge glasshouse originally built at Coulport on the Firth of Clyde in 1860 by the eccentric engineer John Kibble. It was moved to its present site in 1873 — allegedly on a raft towed by a puffer. Retrace your steps to Hillhead Underground when you have done justice to this fascinating location.

Fountain in Kelvingrove Park

The Tenement House

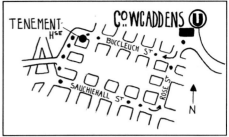

In the eyes of many people, the tenement is synonymous with Glasgow — and with slums. A visit to the Tenement House in Buccleuch Street, which offers a fascinating and authentic record of life earlier this century, should dispel this myth. Many Scottish towns had tenements, and some of the Glaswegian examples bore no more resemblance to slums than a Rolls-Royce does to a banger. In Maxwell Park and Pollokshields, for example, large tenement flats (visible from the Cathcart Circle railway) boasted maids' rooms, some of which, presumably, *were* occupied by maids. Only a few miles away, families were living six to a one-roomed flat, with a shared toilet and all the forms of misery and oppression which sordid living conditions bring.

As Glasgow grew during the industrial revolution, Irish and Highland immigrants flooded into the city to find work, and houses had to be provided. The tenements were built by speculators, by small businessmen seeking an investment, by bodies such as the City Improvement Trust and the Glasgow Workmen's Dwellings Company and by local building societies. Many streets of tenements around large industrial concerns were built — often to quite a high standard — to house that company's workers.

From the early 1890s, red sandstone from Ayrshire and Dumfriesshire became the more common building material, as supplies of local white stone were worked out. The tenements became bigger, better appointed and moved out to the suburbs. To live up a tiled close became the pinnacle of many a Glaswegian's ambitions.

The final large-scale tenement construction took place in Hyndland in the early 1900s; it is still effectively an all-tenement district. By 1910 it was all over.

Mass housing tended to be low-rise until the sprawling estates of the 1950s and 60s, when tens of thousands of people were moved into what they perceived as miles from anywhere with few or no shopping or leisure facilities. Then there were the multi-storey blocks, which merely concentrated people vertically instead of horizontally.

At the same time Glasgow Corporation embarked upon a rapid programme of demolition, believing it could, with the tenements, bulldoze most of the city's ills at the same time. By the time a halt was called, some fine examples had gone and some of what survived was less than ideal.

The trend now is to refurbish tenements rather than remove them. It is now acknowledged that tower blocks and families do not mix — quite an admission from the city which built the 30-storey Red Road flats, the highest domestic housing in Europe.

Meanwhile, just about every type of building from fire stations to warehouses is being turned into flats and new private housing is going up in previously unthinkable areas. Life is returning; the spirit of the tenement lives on.

To visit the Tenement House from Cowcaddens Underground, turn right out of the station, right out of the underpass and left into Rose Street then right into Buccleuch Street. Continue to number 145, at the far end. This tenement close is the location of a remarkable piece of social history: the house in which time stood still. In 1911 a girl called Agnes Toward and her mother moved into one of the flats in the building. Agnes Toward lived in the flat until 1965 — and threw out practically nothing. Everyday items which people would normally discard as outmoded, outdated or simply just unwanted were kept, building up to a fascinating record of Agnes Toward's life — and of that of everyday people at the time.

The flat and its contents were bought by a Scottish actress, Anna Davidson, who later sold them to the National Trust for Scotland which restored the gas lighting, the replacement of which by electricity was one of the few alterations made during Miss Toward's lifetime. Most of the furniture was hers.

The flat consists of a hall, bathroom, bedroom, parlour and kitchen and was built in 1892 which is getting on towards the end of the tenement-building era. In its day it would have been considered superior accommodation. In its present role for the NTS, it has an air of authenticity that no museum, no matter how hard it tries, can ever match. Almost everyone can find something in it to which they can relate. It should not be missed. *Enquiries to (041) 333 0183.*

Turn left on leaving Number 145 and follow the path alongside the M8 slip road to what is left of Charing Cross. As someone said of the city planners: "They knocked down Charing Cross and built a hole in the ground." Charing Cross Mansions, on the Sauchiehall Street corner, need to be seen from the other side of the road to be appreciated. Visible across the motorway is the Mitchell Library, one of several city buildings which are even more impressive when seen floodlit.

Stroll along Sauchiehall Street, passing on the left the regimental museum of the Royal Highland Fusiliers at number 518; the Third Eye Centre, a multi-purpose arts complex at number 350; and the McLellan Galleries at number 270. Turn left into Rose Street to return to Cowcaddens Underground. ❑

Dumbarton Road tenements, Glasgow

Museum and gallery trail

A chance to discover why Glasgow earned its title as the 1990 European City of Culture with a walk which takes in some of the world's finest art and museum collections. Allow plenty of time. (Approx. three miles). See also University and Museums underground trail.

FROM Pollokshaws West station, served by trains to East Kilbride and Barrhead from Glasgow Central, turn left and left again into the entrance to Pollok Estate. The parklands, with Pollok House and its magnificent art collection, were gifted to the city of Glasgow in 1967 by Mrs Anne Maxwell Macdonald, daughter of Sir John Stirling Maxwell, the 10th baronet, and in whose family the lands had been since the 13th century.

Begin walking up the main drive, past Shawmuir Lodge, and branch off to the left, going between the White Cart Water and the tennis courts, cricket ground and police horse and dog training centre. Visible among riverside vegetation are the metal supports for a former suspension bridge. Known as the Springy Bridge — for obvious reasons — it was removed in the 1960s. The point at which the yew trees overhang the river is a favourite spot for those hoping to sight a kingfisher.

The group of buildings beside the river includes the original water-powered sawmill, the lade of which is still on the river, and which handled timber from the estate until well into this century. In the 1890s the original wheel was replaced by a turbine which also supplied electricity to the main house. Alongside is the old stable courtyard, in use by the parks department, and once the farm offices and stabling for horses. In the north-east wall of the inner courtyard are marriage stones bearing the inscription "SIM DGB". This was built on the site of the Maxwell family's third castle in the area, which was superseded by the present Pollok House around 1750.

Near the sawmill is the countryside ranger interpretation centre, which contains an ever-changing display of information about the park and its inhabitants. The service is jointly funded by Glasgow District Council and the Countryside Commission for Scotland and ranger-led guided walks take place throughout the year. *More information on (041) 632 9299.*

The path continues past the Nether Pollok estate First World War memorial set into the garden wall and reaches Pollok House, the first phase of which was begun by the architect William Adam in 1747. He died a year later and the project was completed in 1752 by his son John. Sir John Stirling Maxwell commissioned the second phase near the turn of the century, creating the house as it stands today. The entrance hall was added in 1890; the basement corridor, kitchen and courtyard in 1901 and the library and dining room wings in 1908. Sir John was keenly interested in forestry and horticulture and was responsible for much of the tree planting, including the lime avenue in front of the house's main entrance, a gift for his 21st birthday in 1888. He also developed the woodland garden, with its collection of rhododendrons. There is also a two-acre demonstration garden established in the former walled garden in 1975, with the emphasis on growing fruit and vegetables. The original gardeners' bothy has been restored, showing what life was like around 1900.

The house contains the Stirling Maxwell collection of Spanish and other European paintings, furniture, ceramics and silver. When you have viewed it, leave by the courtyard, with the lime avenue in front of you and bear right onto the tarmac road, which should lead you past some of the park's easiest-spotted and most distinctive inhabitants — the Highland cattle. The breed has an association with the Nether Pollok Estate going back more than 160 years and

Glasgow District Council Parks and Recreation Department is now responsible for about 50 animals, kept all year at Pollok and in summer at Dawsholm, Kings, Linn and Tollcross parks. In summer all they require is grass and water! Each year, the best heifers are kept as future breeding stock with the surplus sold, sometimes to Germany and Holland.

Follow the road round to the left which leads to the Burrell Gallery; purpose-built to house one man's art and antiques collection, a task which it fulfils magnificently. The history of what is now one of Scotland's major tourist attractions is fascinating. It begins with wealthy Glasgow shipowner Sir William Burrell (after whom, incidentally, British Rail named a Class 47 locomo-

Haggs Castle museum

tive). Over a period of 80 years, he amassed a remarkable collection of paintings, stained glass, tapestries, medieval sculpture, ceramics and bronzes, for much of the time faithfully recording his purchases in school exercise books. By all accounts he was a shrewd, if circumspect, collector and drove a hard bargain. He was also reluctant to pay what he considered to be over the odds and consequently missed out on desirable pieces. At first he ap-

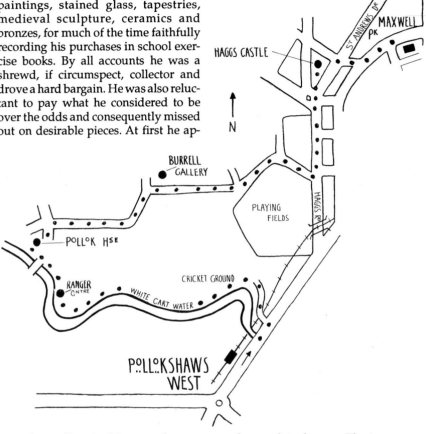

peared to collect for his own pleasure but by the 1930s Sir William was buying with a view to establishing a collection which would at some future date be handed over to public ownership.

In 1944 he took this step, choosing the city of his birth, and subsequently donated £450,000 to build a permanent gallery. However, his conditions were to prove a stumbling block for years to come. Concerned with the smoke pollution prevailing in the city, Sir William stipulated that the gallery should be within four miles of Killearn in Stirlingshire and not less than 16 miles from the Royal Exchange in Glasgow, which did

not leave a lot of scope. The issue was unresolved when he died in 1958, aged 96.

The atmospheric improvements brought about by the introduction of smokeless zones allowed the city to have the conditions altered and the custom-built Burrell Gallery was opened in 1983. In the meantime parts of the 8000-item collection had been on display in such places as Kelvingrove art galleries, although most of it was in store in supposedly secret locations throughout the city.

Architect Barry Gasson has succeeded in making the collection part of the gallery and the gallery part of its surroundings; the glass wall, looking onto mature woods, linking the man-made building with the work of nature. Medieval architectural stonework is an integral part, yet sufficient flexibility is retained to allow changing displays. Admission is free and a visit should not be rushed.

On leaving the building, turn left along the road and left at the junction at the end of the car parking and follow this, the Guidman's Road, to the park exit at Titwood Cottage. Turn left into Haggs Road and at a main junction with traffic lights cross over to St Andrews Drive and the entrance to Haggs Castle museum is on the left.

This is a museum of history, designed expressly for children—although adults ARE admitted — with the emphasis on learning by involvement. It includes a reconstruction of the 16th century kitchen, a 17th century bedroom and the Victorian nursery, plus two exhibition rooms with changing displays.

An inscription above the door records that the castle was built in 1585 — in the traditional L-shape of Scottish tower houses — but what you see today is a 19th century restoration, with an end-of-the-century addition of a new front door, internal staircase and north wing. It was converted into flats then acquired by Glasgow Corporation in 1972 for use as a museum and opened in 1976, following the addition of a new fire stair to the north wing. This was built from reused tenement stone and blends well with the earlier work.

The gardens are an attempt to recreate some features of early gardens, utilising plants typical of the 16th and 17th centuries. This theme extends to the herb and vegetable gardens, which in earlier times would have been a major source of culinary and medicinal ingredients. Today they are used in the museum's activity sessions. A small knot garden, which was a geometric pattern of low clipped hedges or shrubs, has also been included.

Leaflets originally produced soon after the museum opened are still available and entertainingly describe its attractions.

On leaving, cross the road into Terregles Avenue and follow this to Maxwell Park railway station, on the Cathcart Circle route back to Glasgow Central. Note, incidentally, the superior examples of the Glasgow tenement towering over the line. ❏

Charles Rennie Mackintosh trail

A tour around sites connected with Glasgow's famous architect and interior designer.

Glasgow School of Art

TODAY Charles Rennie Mackintosh is celebrated in Glasgow as one of Europe's greatest architects and interior designers. Yet, during his lifetime, Mackintosh achieved little recognition in his own country — although he was acclaimed as a pioneer on the continent.

He was born in 1868, one of 11 children of a police superintendent, and appears to have been determined to pursue an architectural career from an early age. Apprenticed to John Hutchison, he attended evening classes in Glasgow School of Art, which was then located in the Sauchiehall Street building now occupied by the McLellan Galleries. He joined the firm of Honeyman and Keppie as a draughtsman in

1889 and, about the same time, met Herbert McNair and the sisters Margaret and Frances Macdonald. The Four, as they became known, exhibited in craft work and graphic design, in the Art Nouveau style to which Margaret Macdonald, later Mackintosh's wife, remained faithful.

His early work for Honeyman and Keppie shows much restraint, either as a result of his junior position or the client's requirements. The Glasgow Herald building Mitchell Street extension, designed in 1893-94, has Mackintosh touches. Martyr's School, from 1895, is much more identifiably Mackintosh. This was followed by his only church, Queen's Cross, and the nearby but unconnected Ruchill church hall.

In 1896 the governors of Glasgow School of Art invited architectural firms to submit designs for a new building. Honeyman and Keppie's proposal — the work of Mackintosh — was chosen. Shortage of finance resulted in the build-

East gable windows, School of Art

ing being constructed in two phases, over ten years. The eastern section, including the entrance hall, was completed by 1899. Between 1906 and 1907, by which time he had become a partner in Honeyman and Keppie, Mackintosh completely redesigned the planned west wing, which was completed in 1909. This is generally considered to be his finest work, the western gable, with its three tall windows, being especially striking. Internally, the library is hailed as a magnificent achievement.

His other notable buildings included the Daily Record offices in Renfield Lane, Glasgow (1901), The Hill House in Helensburgh (1902-4) and Scotland Street School (1904).

He was also closely associated with the tearooms of Miss Kate Cranston, designing murals for her Buchanan Street premises, furniture for Argyle Street and interiors and furniture for individual sections of the Ingram Street tearooms. Miss Cranston acquired a site in Sauchiehall Street in 1901 and appointed Mackintosh as sole architect, responsible for the building and interiors, of which much of the decorative work is attributed to Margaret Macdonald.

Mackintosh's career peaked with the completion of the School of Art. He undoubtedly suffered conflict with clients whose requirements — and finances — were outstripped by Mackintosh's professional standards. In 1914 he left "the philistines of Glasgow" for Suffolk, moving to London where he was unknown and consequently unemployed, at least as an architect. His last years were spent in France painting watercolours, before returning to London where he died in 1928.

Of what he left behind in Glasgow, the tearooms have fared badly, only the Willow in Sauchiehall Street surviving, after a fashion. His own house in Southpark Avenue was demolished in the

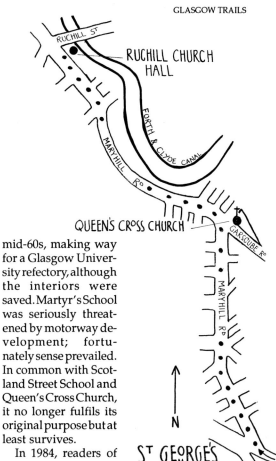

RUCHILL CHURCH HALL

QUEEN'S CROSS CHURCH

N

ST GEORGE'S CROSS

called for a galleried church to seat 700, with a separate hall, linked to the church but accessible from the street, on an cramped corner site with neighbouring buildings inhibiting lighting. The tower has been shown to have been inspired by that of Merriot, Somerset. The interior, especially, displays the architect's attention to detail, particularly in the carving. The building is now the headquarters of the Charles Rennie Mackintosh Society and is usually open Tuesdays, Thursdays, Fridays and Sundays in the afternoon. *Check with (041) 946 6600.*

Continuing along Maryhill Road for a further three-quarters of a mile leads to Ruchill church hall, at the corner of Ruchill Street. Mackintosh was responsible for the 1898 grey sandstone hall, built as a mission for Westbourne Church in Glasgow's West End, but not the church alongside, which is of a later date. The hall is considered a minor work in Mackintosh terms.

mid-60s, making way for a Glasgow University refectory, although the interiors were saved. Martyr's School was seriously threatened by motorway development; fortunately sense prevailed. In common with Scotland Street School and Queen's Cross Church, it no longer fulfils its original purpose but at least survives.

In 1984, readers of *Building Design* magazine voted Mackintosh as the best-known architect and the Glasgow School of Art as the best-known modern building. Of this are reputations, belatedly, made.

This Mackintosh trail breaks into three parts, utilising Underground, feet and trains, and can be done in any order.

From St George's Cross Underground station, turn right at street level and cross the road. Turn left and continue along Maryhill Road for three-quarters of a mile until Queen's Cross Church is reached on the right, at the Garscube Road junction. This was a challenging task for Mackintosh, for the design brief

Return to St George's Cross Underground station, either on foot or by bus (for which the correct fare is required) and alight at Hillhead. Turn left into Byres Road and left again into University Avenue. The Hunterian Art Gallery is on the left at the top of the hill and in it are found reconstructed interiors from 78 Southpark Avenue, Glasgow, Mackintosh's home from 1906-1914. He and his wife made sweeping alterations to the Victorian terraced house, substituting their own decoration and fitments and designing their own furniture. The main bedroom, dining room and studio drawing room have been recreated in the art gallery, whose Mackintosh collection includes more than 60 pieces of furniture and 600 drawings, watercolours and designs, selections of which are on permanent display. *Open weekdays and Saturday mornings; check details with (041) 330 5431.* Do not confuse the Hunterian Art Gallery with the Hunterian Museum, which is on the opposite side of University Avenue.

Leaving the gallery, return to University Avenue and turn left, then right, into Kelvin Way. Before the traffic lights take the entrance leading to the Kelvingrove Art Gallery, where another Mackintosh interior has been reconstructed. This is a section of the Chinese Room of Miss Cranston's Ingram Street tearoom, in which the walls were lined with hessian and painted blue with wooden lattices. The furniture was dark oak; the upholstery and curtains dark blue. The exhibit is part of a gallery devoted to The Glasgow Style, in which Mackintosh's contemporaries in the fields of craft and design are represented.

Leave the Art Gallery by the front

Queen's Cross church

entrance and walk along Dumbarton Road to Kelvinhall Underground, on the right past Byres Road junction. Travel to Shields Road. Across from the Underground station is Scotland Street School, one of Mackintosh's most attractive buildings. It was standard school board practice at the time to insist upon separate entrances for boys and girls so the general plan, with classrooms between the staircases and cloakrooms at each end, was more or less obligatory. The staircase bays, almost entirely glass, are the dominant features of the 1904 building, designed when Mackintosh had achieved partner status and thus had a freer hand. It closed as a school in 1979 and became a museum of education. *Check opening times on (041) 429 1202.*

Take the Underground to St Enoch for section two of the Mackintosh trail — the all-walking part.

At St Enoch, turn left into Argyle Street then immediately right into the narrow Mitchell Street, location of the Glasgow Herald building with which Mackintosh was associated — the unusual treatment of the tower suggests his influence. Continue to Drury Street, where you can visit the Horseshoe Bar. This has nothing to do with Mackintosh but its traditional interior is renowned. Cross Renfield Street into Renfield Lane. Tucked away in this city centre backwater is Mackintosh's Daily Record building of 1901, not to be confused with the Hope Street premises vacated in 1971. It is difficult to appreciate the Renfield

Hunterian art gallery

Lane building, as it is hemmed in on a shadowy street only 18 feet wide. The façade, four storeys of white glazed tile on a grey sandstone base, deserves better. Both of the former Mackintosh newspaper offices are viewable from the outside only.

Walk up Hope Street, at the western end of Renfield Lane, to Sauchiehall Street and turn left. After a short distance, Henderson's the jeweller's is the location of Miss Cranston's Willow tearooms (Sauchiehall means lane of willows), designed internally and externally by Mackintosh. Much was lost after the premises were absorbed into a department store in 1926 but in the late 1970s the frontage and the Room de Luxe were restored, as far as possible, to the original designs. The jeweller's occupies the ground floor while the Room de Luxe is once again a tearoom, with Mackintosh-style furniture.

Head west along Sauchiehall Street to Dalhousie Street on the right and climb the hill to the School of Art on the corner of Renfrew Street. This first phase was criticised for being art nouveau, the stark lines lacking the expected historical features such as columns or pedi-

ments. It, and the subsequent second phase, are now recognised as being the beginning of a new era in architecture. Mackintosh believed that construction should be decorated, and not decoration constructed. The School of Art, possibly more than any other of his buildings, rewards close examination of details, such as the ironwork, the decorations, the interior use of materials in their raw state and the creation of light and images of space.

The school also contains architectural drawings, watercolours and furniture from other Mackintosh commissions, displayed in the Mackintosh room and the Furniture Gallery. *Enquiries about opening times should be made to (041) 332 9797.*

The third part of the trail links the unlikely combination of Martyr's School and The Hill House in Helensburgh, although they can be visited separately.

Taking as a notional starting point the Dundas Street entrance to Queen Street station (beside which is also a Buchanan Street Underground entrance), walk up Dundas Street and turn right into Cathedral Street. Continue past college and university buildings and bear left into

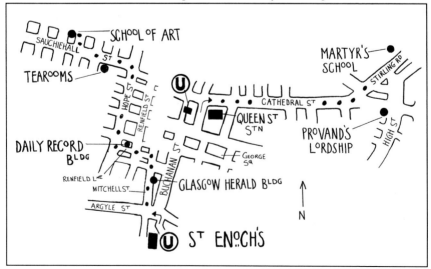

Stirling Road. The school can be seen to the north of the street, before the motorway slip road. Walking distance is about three-quarters of a mile.

This Honeyman and Keppie commission, designed in 1895, is identifiably Mackintosh in the decorative treatment of the main entrance, the tall windows and, internally, the exposed wooden roof beams and trusses. As was the case in the later Scotland Street School, the requirement for segregation of the sexes influenced the general layout. The building ceased to be a school in 1976, as its catchment area had disappeared under motorways, and following renovation has become the Forum arts centre, *open to visitors only by arrangement with the administrator (041 552 2104)*. Incidentally, the Gothic building opposite is St Mungo's Retreat, dating from 1890-2.

Either retrace your steps to Queen Street station or cross Stirling Road into the short Glebe Street then right and down Castle Street passing Provands Lordship and Glasgow Cathedral and High Street *(see East city trail)* to High Street station. At either station, board a train for Helensburgh.

At Helensburgh Central, turn right then sharp right into Sinclair Street, walking up to Kennedy Drive on the left. Then turn right into Upper Colquhoun Street, in which The Hill House is situated. The distance is about a mile, mostly uphill. Helensburgh Upper station, on the West Highland line, is encountered on the way.

Occupying a commanding site, the house was designed and built for the publisher Walter Blackie, between 1902 and 1904. It has overtones of the Scottish baronial style which appealed to Mackintosh, particularly in the use of turret staircases. He designed fireplaces, furniture and fittings, right down to pewter fire tongs, and even made alterations to accommodate a nursery, for an unexpected addition to the client's family. From private hands, The Hill House passed into the care of the Royal Incorporation of Architects in Scotland and, in 1982, became National Trust for Scotland property. *Enquiries to (0436) 73900.* Return by way of Helensburgh Central, or Helensburgh Upper, if the West Highland Line timetable permits. ❑

MACKINTOSH TRAIL
Telephone numbers

Queen's Cross Church (headquarters of the Charles Rennie Mackintosh society): 041 946 6600
Glasgow School of Art: 041 332 9797
Hunterian Art Gallery: 041 330 5431
Scotland Street School: 041 429 1202
Willow tearooms: 041 332 0521
Ruchill church hall: 041 946 0466
Martyr's School: 041 552 2104
Kelvingrove Art Gallery: 041 357 3929
The Hill House: 0436 73900

NOTE: Scheduled for opening in late 1990 was the **Art Lover's House**, a design submitted by Mackintosh for a competition in Germany in 1901, which is being created in Glasgow's Bellahouston park. It combines office use and accessibility to the public.

Springburn

Today there is little left in Springburn to show it for what it once was — the world capital of locomotive construction. The following is not so much a trail as a tribute to this once thriving suburb.

THIRTY years ago, the northern Glasgow suburb of Springburn was a thriving, bustling community, whose past, present and — as it turned out — future revolved round the railway locomotive. Within its boundaries were two major British Railways workshops — Cowlairs and St Rollox — and the Hyde Park and Atlas works of the privately-owned North British Locomotive Company and Eastfield locomotive shed. For the inhabitants of the district, the day was ruled by the works horn; their milk came in bottles with a railway locomotive emblem, they shopped at Cowlairs Co-op, founded by North British Railway workers — in fact, almost every aspect of their lives had its origins with one of the railway employers. It was not a company town but it was a community, in every sense of the word. It was an honest, self-reliant, working-class district, one of many in the West of Scotland. And like so many other places, Springburn was destroyed.

It began with the decline of basic

Sudan Railways 4-8-2 locomotive — one of 42 built at Springburn's Hyde Park Works in the early fifties — leaves Vulcan Street en route for the docks

industries. Of course, Springburn had known lean times, the NB Loco in particular being hit by the depression of the late 1920s and 1930s. The Atlas works, for instance, were closed in 1923 and reopened only because of World War Two munitions work. In 1933 the Combine, as it was known, built only 16 locomotives and this included its Queens Park works in the city's south side.

In 1962, the NB Loco went into liquidation, after a decade of poor results exacerbated by an unsuccessful attempt to make the transition from steam to diesel. Cowlairs railway workshops closed in 1966, some men transferring to St Rollox which over the years was steadily downgraded and is now a repair depot for British Rail Maintenance Ltd, with a much-reduced workforce. Other employers such as Braby's ironworks and the Saracen Foundry, in nearby Possilpark, also disappeared.

Employment was the mortar which held the bricks of a community together, but the break-up was assisted by the city fathers who embarked upon a programme of tenement demolition and construction of high-density housing, allied to an expressway plan which took 25 years to come anywhere near completion. At one and the same time, the physical appearance of the district was being changed beyond recognition; people were moving out in search of work and others were moving in, having been allocated houses. The cinemas closed; the shops, including the Co-op, were demolished; schools, churches, the pleasure garden, pubs, cafés — almost everything people could remember and identify with — fell victim to the bull-

dozer.

All of which helps to explain why there is so little remaining of Springburn's railway heritage. Of Cowlairs works, there is a gatepost, if you know where to look. (It's not worth the effort.) Of the North British Locomotive Company's Hyde Park works, there are two gates, one of them tucked away at a relatively inaccessible end of Flemington Street, next to the railway. In the same street is the company's former office block, now a technical college. Built around a quadrangle, it is a listed building and retains its three magnificent war memorial stained glass windows and the top floor drawing office, with its excellent natural lighting. In stone above the main door, on either side of a railway locomotive, are the female figures of Speed and Science. This is not the only surviving example of railway sculpture; on the sadly-decrepit public hall at the corner of Keppochill Road and Millarbank Street is a Greek goddess cradling a locomotive in her arms.

The Atlas has gone, only its name being perpetuated in an industrial estate. The former office block of St Rollox works in Springburn Road still stands but is not part of the BRML complex.

Most of the works area, plus the former Sighthill goods depot, is earmarked for redevelopment. Further down Springburn Road, towards the city centre, the railway bridge which was a successor to the Garnkirk and Glasgow Railway's Inchbelly Bridge and which carried a mineral line into Port Dundas, was removed in 1989 as part of road improvements.

Springburn railway station, built in 1885 for the City of Glasgow Union Railway, is still there, terminus of a north bank electric route and also served by Cumbernauld line trains from Glasgow Queen Street high level. Adjacent to it is the one good reason for going to Springburn — the local museum housed in a library building, the land for which was donated in 1902 by Neilson, Reid and Company, one of the constituents of the NB Loco. Founded in 1986, it was Glasgow's first community museum and has railway-orientated displays as well as changing exhibitions, mostly related to social conditions. Great emphasis has been placed on recording history through the words and memories of local people.

Opposite the museum, a laid-out square was constructed in 1988, on part of the site of the Hyde Park works. The vast area had lain derelict for more than 20 years until house building began on it in 1989. It is new housing such as this and other recent developments that give hope for the future; that life will return to the heart of Springburn. Even the former fire station and labour exchange have been converted into flats. ❑

Coast and country

Auld Brig o' Doon, Alloway — see Burns trail

The Strathclyde region may incorporate one of Britain's largest conurbations, but it also boasts some of its most stunning scenery. The following walks take you through some of it — starting at Ardlui at the northern tip of Loch Lomond then roughly following the line of the Clyde down the coast to Culzean

Loch Lomond: north

ARDLUI — INVERARNAN — ARDLEISH

This walk takes you to the northern limit of the Strathclyde PTE Day Tripper ticket and gives plenty of opportunities to admire the surrounding scenery. Around 9 miles return — distance halved if ferry used.

Ardlui

THE hamlet of Ardlui, at the head of Loch Lomond, consists of a railway station, hotel, campsite, a handful of houses and a pier. A popular post-war circular tour from Glasgow, utilising train and steamer, ran until 1964 when Ardlui pier was closed. The station is noteworthy in that the main buildings had to be demolished in 1970, following subsidence. They were similar to other West Highland Line stations, being of the typical Swiss chalet style.

The River Falloch, which flows into the loch at Ardlui, was canalised in the mid-19th century as far as Inverarnan, where steamers connected with stagecoaches at the hotel. Once a cattle drovers' inn and later a favourite haunt of

generations of hillwalkers and climbers, it still stands.

To reach Inverarnan from Ardlui station, turn left coming out of the station underpass and walk along the A82, taking due care with the traffic. The hotel is reached after two miles; a few hundred yards past it on the right is a bridge over the River Falloch. Cross this, pausing to admire the waterfall of the Ben Glas Burn hopefully tumbling down the hillside, then go right, over a stile, and continue heading south as far as the Ben Glas Burn itself, which marks the boundary between the Strathclyde and Central Regions. Over another stile, cross the burn by a footbridge built by the Royal Engineers and follow the West

Highland Way, passing the ruined hamlet of Blairstainge, proof that this part of the world once supported a greater population than it does now.

Swing round and look northwards, for views of Ben Lui and Ben Oss. Beyond the reedy Dubh Lochan — the Little Black Loch — and a little to the west of the path, the magnificent viewpoint of Cnap Mor is reached, which gives a vista of Loch Lomond writhing southwards with Ben Lomond prominent on the left. This marks the start of the Loch Lomond section of the 95-mile West Highland Way, which runs from Milngavie, on the outskirts of Scotland's largest city, to Fort William, at the foot of Scotland's highest mountain. A word of warning — the popularity of the Way has created a major erosion problem and some parts can be wet underfoot.

After another half-mile, the wooded shore of Loch Lomond is reached at Ardleish, where a signal hoist can be used to summon and hire a ferry boat back to Ardlui; retracing your steps is, of course, an alternative to using the boat. In any case, it would be best to check out the availability of the ferry before setting out. ❑

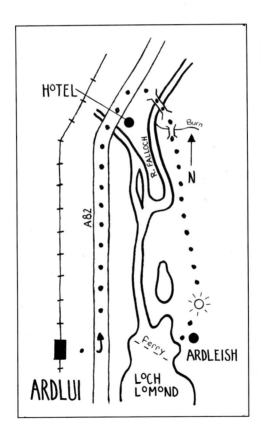

Loch Lomond: south

*Scenic walk around the southern tip of
Loch Lomond. (Approx. 3½ miles)*

BALLOCH lies at the end of an single-track branch on the north suburban electric network at the end of Loch Lomond.

Until 1986, the railway extended to the lochside at Balloch Pier station, serving for many years the state-owned paddle steamer *Maid of the Loch*. Following the withdrawal and sale of the vessel, due to the declining interest in cruising, the smaller *Countess Fiona* appeared on the loch. Most of its passengers, by all accounts, were from cars.

It was no surprise when closure notices for the half-mile pier branch appeared towards the end of 1985. A major attraction of such action, from an operational point of view, was that it would remove the need for a level crossing over the main road, if Balloch Central station was relocated.

The last train from Balloch Pier ran on Sunday September 28, 1986, when unit 303068 formed the 15.39 departure to Dumbarton Central. The occasion went largely unnoticed by anyone other than

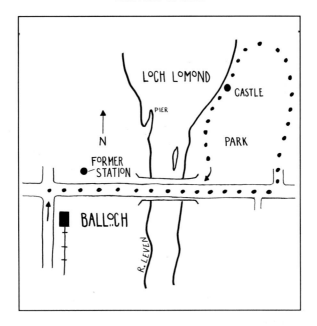

a handful of railway enthusiasts and a slightly bemused driver and guard. In April 1988, a new station, on the Glasgow side of the road, was brought into use and the original Balloch Central, with its level crossing and gatebox, was closed. The main building, stone-cleaned and renovated, has been retained as a tourist centre.

On arrival at Balloch, turn right into the main road, cross the River Leven and continue to the gates of Balloch Castle Country Park, on the left. All that remains of the 1238 castle, ancient seat of the Earls of Lennox, is a mound and depression which formed the moat. Old Balloch Castle had a relatively short life, as the Lennoxes moved to a safer site on an island in Loch Lomond. The present Balloch Castle — now a visitor centre — incorporated stone from the 13th century structure. The main drive leads to the visitor centre, occupying a commanding position overlooking the loch.

From the centre, take the path heading north, which has the car park on the right. Look out for a headstone between the car park and the path, marking the grave of Bran, a family pet who died in 1883. The walk is essentially a stroll through a public park with the loch visible through the trees in places. The path curves round towards the lochside, leads to the river bank and emerges at a grassy area, overlooking a river packed with boats. Cross the river and walk back to the station, which makes a total distance of about 3$^1/_2$ miles.

Alternatively, a cycle route which runs along the western bank of the River Leven can be followed to Alexandria, Renton or Dalreoch stations. The distance from Balloch to Dalreoch is four miles. ❑

Left: Sunset over Loch Lomond with an old slipway gantry in silhouette

The South Clyde

LANGBANK — PORT-GLASGOW — GREENOCK

Several reminders of the Clyde's mighty maritime past are recalled in this varied walk which also takes in the home of the chief of the MacMillan clan, and Newark Castle, once visited by James IV. (Approx. six miles of walking)

TAKE a Wemyss Bay or Gourock-bound electric train from Glasgow or Paisley and alight at Langbank. On leaving the station turn left along the village main street and continue westward for under a mile, until the entrance to Finlaystone Estate is reached. There are several woodland walks, gardens with fine views of the Clyde Estuary and adventure playgrounds.

The house, home of the Cunninghams, Earls of Glencairn, for 500 years, has associations with Robert Burns and 16th century historian and theologican, John Knox. It is now a centre for the clan MacMillan, being the home of its chief. There is a fine collection of international dolls. Finlaystone House tends to be open on Sundays from April to August.

Check on Langbank (047 554) 285.

Return to the station and pick up a westbound train to Port Glasgow, where a castle can be found hidden behind a shipyard. This is Newark Castle, which is reached by going straight down John Wood Street, behind the steeple and right into the main road. Cross at a convenient point and access to the castle is near the roundabout, behind Ferguson's shipyard. Newark, which is remarkably well preserved, has many corner turrets and a stair tower. The tower was built between 1450 and 1477 and the central building completed in 1799.

Right: Newark castle pictured just before the turn of this century. The shipyard on the left was in use in one form or another since the mid-18th century

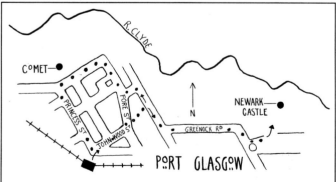

74

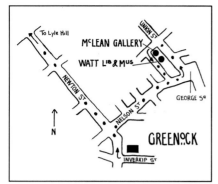

It is considered to be a fine example of the development of the French style of architecture in Scotland in the 17th century.

The castle was visited by James IV in 1495, on his way to the Western Highlands. He would at least have been able to communicate, as he was the last Scots king to "have the Gaelic".

Return along the main road to the replica of Henry Bell's *Comet*, in its own watery location. It was built in 1962 at Lithgow's East Yard to mark the 150th anniversary of the launching of the original *Comet*, the first Clyde passenger steamer. On trials, the *Comet* travelled from Glasgow to Greenock in three and a half hours and later pioneered the Glasgow to the Western Highlands route. She met her end on the rocks at Craignish Point in Argyll in 1820; fortunately the engine was saved, ending up in the collection of the Science Museum in London. The replica suffered a kinder fate, sailing to Helensburgh and back before being laid up. Make your way back to the railway station by Princes Street, on the right hand side of the modern building opposite the *Comet*. Despite the face it presents to the main street, the station itself retains its traditional air.

The same can be said of Greenock Central, which is worth a stop for its own sake. Nearby is the refurbished Custom House, embarkation point for many North American emigrants, and now home of an exhibition on the work of Customs and Excise. No doubt the building will be enhanced once the waterfront redevelopment of the Greenock area improves the surroundings.

Back to the train and Greenock West is the station for an adventurous trek to the Lyle Hill, site of the Free French memorial, imaginatively combining the Cross of Lorraine and an anchor, which pays tribute to the French sailors who died in the Battle of the Atlantic. It is $1\frac{1}{2}$ miles uphill to the memorial but the spectacular views from Lyle Hill make the effort worthwhile. On leaving Greenock West, turn right and continue along Newton Street to your goal. Retrace your steps and at the junction of Newton Street and Nelson Street turn left, then left into Union Street at George Square. On the left is the Watt Monument Museum and, round the corner in Kelly Street, the McLean Museum and Art Gallery, which houses material relating to the social, industrial and maritime history of the area, plus a collection of paintings by Scottish artists. Return to your starting point by the same route.❑

Greenock Cut

This trail follows the line of an old aqueduct system which used to supply Greenock with water. A walk along it provides stunning views of the Firth of Clyde and surrounding area.
(Approx. seven miles — alternative routes can make up a longer walk.)

THIS lengthy trail begins at Greenock West station. Cross Inverkip Street and the road which runs parallel to it and walk up Mount Pleasant Street, crossing intersecting roads until Prospecthill Street is reached. Turn right along it and then left opposite Cowdenknowes Reservoir and continue uphill, crossing the main road and passing houses built in memory of the dead of the First World War. Bear right at T-junction and then take the road signposted The Cut. Just before some houses, a road on the left leads to a small car park at Overton cottage. It is a mile from the station but being all uphill, the distance may seem longer.

At the cottage, take the right-hand track which follows the Greenock Cut, part of a remarkable supply system built in the 1820s to provide Greenock with water for domestic and industrial purposes. The cut, clay-lined and clinging to the hill face, carried water from Loch Thom reservoir, named after Robert Thom, who designed and built the aqueduct system, which is no longer in use. The walk alongside it, with the cut on your left, gives superb views over the Firth of Clyde to the Cowal Peninsula and up Loch Long, with the Cobbler at its head.

The way swings east below Dunrod hill, past Shielhill Farm, across the road and past the headwater pool for the Greenock Cut, arriving at Cornalees Bridge visitor centre, which houses the ranger's office, toilets and a display about the area. (There is also the engine of a training aircraft which crashed on Dunrod Hill in 1939.) Here there is a choice of routes. Heading north from the visitor centre, past the Compensation reservoir on the right and skirting Loch Thom, leads across moorland back to Overton cottage. *The distance for this circle is about seven miles.*

Alternatively, walk back over the modern bridge and cross the spillway, down which excess water from Loch Thom and the Compensation reservoir can be lead into the Kip Water. Turn right along the Kelly Cut, which brought water from the Kelly reservoir to the Compensation reservoir. Once again, a panorama of the Firth of Clyde unfolds as you make your way along the cut. Before the Kelly reservoir, turn right and, keeping the Kelly Burn on the left, continue to a water board road which emerges at a rather unattractive caravan site, on the right. This road continues round the rear of another caravan park (which stretches all the way down to the coast at Wemyss Bay) and after half a mile crosses the railway line outside Wemyss Bay. Turn left at the main road and Wemyss Bay station is reached in just over half a mile. *The distance from Cornalees Bridge to Wemyss Bay by this route is about six miles.* Another alternative involves the start of the route, which is part of a nature trail. This branches away from the Kelly Cut and into wooded Shielhill Glen, on a board-walk across moorland on which grouse are reared, hence the hides used during the shooting season. The glen has been

designated a Site of Special Scientific Interest, chiefly because of its natural hardwood content. The nature trail emerges from the glen at the Greenock Cut and follows it as previously described to the visitor centre.

A return by way of Inverkip station, some $3\frac{1}{2}$ miles distant, can be made by following the tarmac road through Shielhill Farm. The route is all downhill and prominent ahead is the chimney of Inverkip power station. Take the left fork after about $1\frac{1}{2}$ miles and you eventually arrive in Inverkip main

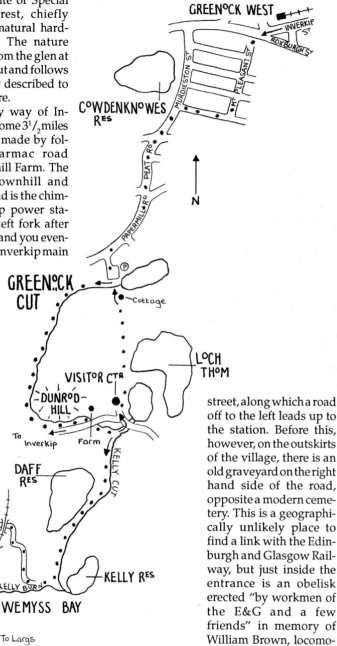

street, along which a road off to the left leads up to the station. Before this, however, on the outskirts of the village, there is an old graveyard on the right hand side of the road, opposite a modern cemetery. This is a geographically unlikely place to find a link with the Edinburgh and Glasgow Railway, but just inside the entrance is an obelisk erected "by workmen of the E&G and a few friends" in memory of William Brown, locomotive superintendent who died in 1864, aged 29. ❑

Left: Loch Long and the Cobbler

Wemyss Bay to Largs

Most of this walk is around the town of Largs — although it can be extended with a visit to Kelburn Country Park. (Approx. one and a half miles.)

WEMYSS Bay station, one of the destinations of the previous chapter's walk, is worth revisiting in its own right. It is at the end of the route from Glasgow Central and still manages to capture some of the atmosphere of the heyday of *Doon the Watter*, when vast crowds of industrial workers and their families poured off trains and onto Rothesay-bound steamers. Today the crowds sit in airport lounges, the trains are electric and the boat is a car ferry. The 1903 station remains however. It is still possible to stand at Wemyss Bay, with its wide ramp to the pier, and curved surfaces to ease passenger flow, and imagine how it once was.

Outside the station, cross the main road and catch a bus to Largs, a bustling resort and residential town sandwiched between the Firth of Clyde and high ground to the east. It is opposite the Isles of Cumbrae, for which it is the ferry point. Cross the road at the pedestrian crossing outside the station and turn left. Continue to the entrance next to the George Hotel and turn right. Here you will find the Largs local history museum next to an old graveyard, in which is situated the Skelmorlie Aisle, a mausoleum and all that survives of the Old Kirk of Largs which was demolished in 1802. The burial aisle was built in 1636 by Sir Robert Montgomery of Skelmorlie, whose lead coffin, along with that of his wife Margaret, who was allegedly killed by a kick from her horse, still lies there.

The elaborate carved stone tomb is without parallel in Scotland and is an ancient monument, with a custodian on duty from April to September. The painted ceiling is of particular interest and includes a representation of the building before the church was demolished.

Also to be found in the graveyard is the burial vault of the Brisbane family, of whom Sir Thomas Brisbane gave his name to the capital of New South Wales, Australia. Between the Brisbane vault and the graveyard wall is a reconstructed Bronze Age cist (burial chamber), of the kind found elsewhere in the area.

Return to the main street, cross into Bath Street and continue along the sea front, over the bridge across the Gogo River and encountering on the left the Christian Heritage Museum in Mackerston Place. Further along, residential flats now occupy the site of the Marine and Curlinghall Hotel, whose gateway survives as a reminder. The beachside path leads to The Pencil, a monument, erected in 1912, to commemorate the Battle of Largs in 1263, when Alexander the Third defeated the gale-battered fleet of Norse king Haakon. As a result of this, the Hebrides became part of Scotland. Each year the town holds a Viking festival which attracts Scandinavians with more peaceful intentions.

Retrace your steps, cross the railway line by the footbridge and walk along Walkerston Avenue, then right into Anthony Road and left into Irvine Road. Douglas Park is the home of the Burns Garden, which features plants and shrubs mentioned in the poet's works. Also in the park is the Haylie Chambered Tomb, dating from pre-3000BC. A

The Pencil, Largs

detour on the way leads to a fine view over the town towards the Cumbraes and beyond. Return to the main road, turn right and make your way back to the railway station.

Kelburn Country Park, on the A78 between Largs and Fairlie, is also well worth a visit. It is two miles from Largs — turn right outside the station and start walking or enquire at the bus station about service buses. Alternatively, a minibus service operates to and from Largs station. *(In 1990 departures from Largs were at 1145 and 1345 but telephone 0475 568685 or 568554 to check.)*

On arrival, by whatever means you choose, you will find excellent walks ranging from a half-hour stroll to a two and a half hour expedition. The most rewarding is probably the Long Glen Walk which goes to the top of Kelburn Glen and affords magnificent views over the Firth of Clyde. Go up by the South Glen Path and descend by the much-steeper North Glen Path. The distance is only one and a half miles but a 500 foot climb makes the walk more of a chal-

lenge than it may look.

For continuous views of the Firth, the Countess's Walk is recommended. It heads northwards from the castle gardens to meet the Upper Estate Road, from which point there is a superb view towards Ayr, with the Mull of Kintyre and Ailsa Craig visible on a clear day.

Following the road round to descend by the Corkscrew Road should give a not-too-demanding walk lasting about one and a half hours.

Sedate walking can be had through the gardens, created over the centuries and featuring rare and exotic plants and trees. Kelburn is the home of the Earls of Glasgow and the Seventh Earl's Governorship of New Zealand from 1892-97 has resulted in a museum of his South Pacific curiosities, as well as a garden of New Zealand plants.

Other Kelburn attractions include a genuine Commando assault course (fit adults only please!); a less strenuous children's adventure course; pets' corner; riding centre and ranger service. Kelburn Castle, the family home of the

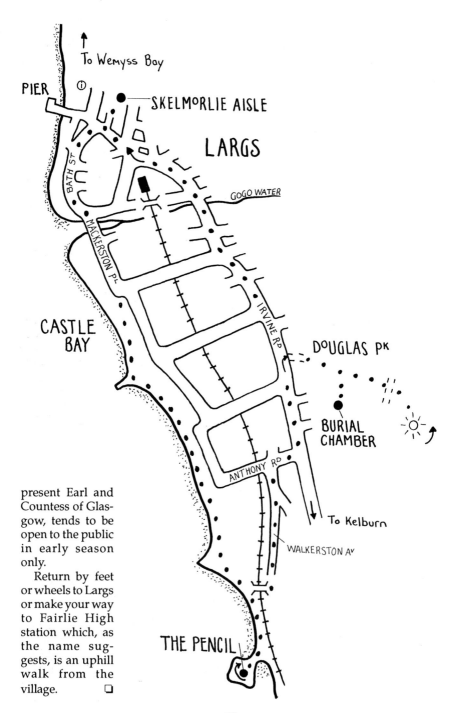

To Wemyss Bay

PIER

SKELMORLIE AISLE

LARGS

BATH ST

MACKERSTON PL

GOGO WATER

CASTLE
BAY

IRVINE RD

DOUGLAS PK

BURIAL
CHAMBER

ANTHONY RD

To Kelburn

WALKERSTON AV

THE PENCIL

present Earl and
Countess of Glasgow, tends to be
open to the public
in early season
only.

Return by feet
or wheels to Largs
or make your way
to Fairlie High
station which, as
the name suggests, is an uphill
walk from the
village. ❏

Lochwinnoch to Windy Hill

The walk takes in a bird reserve, fine river scenery, a country park and a hill with superb panoramic views. (A ten mile walk. Allow five hours.)

THIS walk starts and finishes at Lochwinnoch Station on the Glasgow-Ayr line, which has an excellent 30-minute service, even on Sundays. It climbs to just over 1000 feet at its highest point, and even though most of it is on lanes, it is a very pleasant and varied walk with superb views in clear conditions.

All of the country traversed is within the Clyde Muirshiel Regional Park, an exercise in co-operative land management and one of four such parks so far established in Scotland. Although the informative booklet on the regional park says that it "has much in common with a national park, both in the kind of provision for recreation and the value placed on the scenery", this appears to be working against the walker in Clyde Muirshiel.

Indeed, a little further on the booklet says that "too much disturbance can ruin the very beauty that people come to see, and so entry is limited to those areas in which there is no conflict of interest". The real conflict of interest, it could be suggested, is with landowners over both sheep farming and grouse shooting, and notices at Muirshiel Country Park reinforce this point. To avoid placing readers of this book in difficult situations, the route has been confined to "safe" ground; but it is to be hoped in the not too distant future that much more of the fine wild moorland north of Lochwinnoch is opened up to proper public access.

Walk down the station access road, and if you wish, cross the A760 with care

Craig Minnan seen from Windy Hill

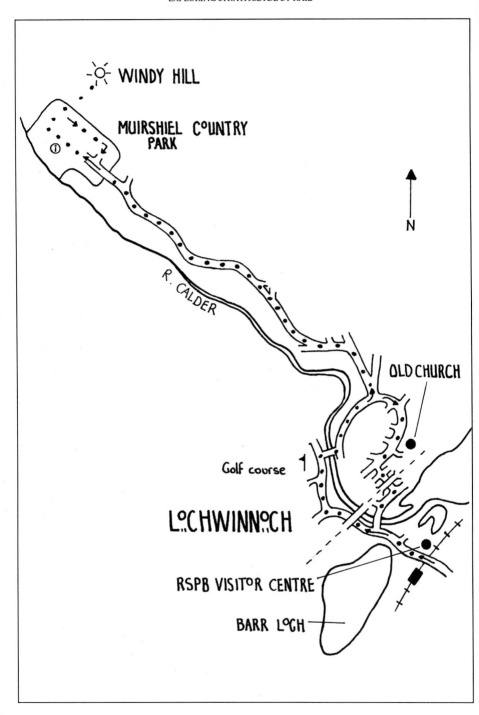

and visit the RSPB bird reserve directly opposite. There is a visitor centre with an observation tower and you can walk out to hides overlooking the loch. The birdlife here is fascinating at all times of the year, and in winter the wildfowl and wading birds are very fine.

Continue along the main road, effectively a causeway dividing Barr Loch and Castle Semple Loch. The westward views across Barr Loch attract both the eye and the camera. At Garthland Lodge cross the road to stay on the pavement and walk along beside the River Calder to enter the village of Lochwinnoch. Take the second road on the right (Burnfoot Road, not the B786 signposted for Muirshiel Country Park) and walk beneath fine horse chestnut trees to reach Lochwinnoch Golf Club, a pleasantly wooded course that spreads up the hill on the left.

Continue along the lane, with the river chuckling by on the right, to a junction. Turn right past a very attractive group of houses, cross the river and continue uphill on the lane, shortly passing a weir on the river.

Soon after this a gap in the wall on the left shows an inviting-looking path running beside the river. A diversion can be made here, but unfortunately the path peters out and does not provide a riverside walk to the country park. In time, it is hoped that the path can be extended, but for now you can enjoy a short walk beside the river through (in spring) a mass of bluebells, before returning to the lane.

Turn left at the B786 and immediately left again (signposted to Muirshiel Country Park). This lane is followed for three miles as it winds steadily uphill. It passes a number of attractive houses and farms, Clovenstone being perhaps the nicest, and as you climb, the views around you steadily open out and become more interesting. The Calder is seen emerging from its gorge and running through a wide valley, with Misty Law prominent above it. A little further west is the source of the River Garnock, whose estuary you meet in the Ayrshire Coast walk on page 87.

Shortly after passing the ruined farm of Heathfield, you reach the entrance gates for Muirshiel Country Park. The park, which covers the former policies of Muirshiel Estate, was opened in 1970 as a contribution to European Conservation Year. It is at the centre of a most interesting area, for surprising reasons.

The area has connections with Covenanters, whose Protestant beliefs brought them into conflict with the Crown in the 17th century. Craig Minnan, to the north-east, was used as a lookout post, and James Renwick, Scotland's last religious martyr, addressed open-air meetings, or "coventicles", hereabouts. He was executed in Edinburgh in 1688 for his beliefs.

Above the park, on Queenside Muir, was a mine producing barytes, used in barium meal X-rays and as a constituent of cosmetics, paper and toothpaste. At its peak in the 1960s it turned out 17,000 tons a year and reached 800 feet below ground. Muirshiel House, built here in the 19th century, was demolished in the 1950s and nothing remains today except the name.

Perhaps strangest of all is the reputation the area has earned as Renfrewshire's "Bermuda Triangle". There have been more than 20 aircraft crashes on these moors in the past 50 years, and remains are to be seen at a number of places.

Today, Muirshiel Country Park has trails winding down to the River Calder, around the woodland, and up to Windy Hill. There is extensive birdlife and the small visitor centre has excellent displays explaining more, and a helpful staff of rangers. Leaflets are freely available.

Before starting the return journey, take

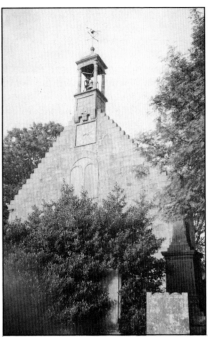

The rocky gorge of the River Calder near Lochwinnoch

Tower of the old church at Lochwinnoch, dated 1727

the short walk up to Windy Hill on a signposted path (mostly on a boardwalk). From the summit, the site of an Iron Age "roundhouse" in around 1000BC, the panorama is magnificent, with Ben Lomond clearly visible to the north and the town of Kilmacolm nearer at hand. A short distance away to the east is Craig Minnan, its sharp peak making it clear why it was valued by the Covenanters as a lookout post.

Return to the park and start back down the lane. The outward route is taken as far as the B786, but then take this road down into Lochwinnoch. Where the main street starts is the tower of the old church, dated 1727 on the lintel and with its clock stuck at ten past ten.

You can either walk down the main street (in which there is a local history museum) or take the first turning left (St Winnoc Road) and follow it round be-

side Castle Semple Loch, where you may well see windsurfing, canoeing and sailing as well as the ever-patient anglers. The road becomes Lochlip Road and is briefly part of the Glasgow-Irvine cycle route, recently opened.

The outward route is rejoined at the pleasant bridge over the River Calder, from where it is a short walk back to Lochwinnoch Station.

The RSPB Visitor Centre is open Thursday to Sunday, 10am to 5pm. Castle Semple and Muirshiel Country Parks are open daily during daylight hours. Information leaflets are available at all three places. ❑

The Ayrshire coast

IRVINE TO TROON

This walk takes in a fascinating museum, a glorious stretch of coast, golf courses, and a marina. (Seven miles — allow three hours.)

BEFORE the advent of the package holiday, many thousands of Glasgow families took their annual holiday on the Ayrshire coast. Today, the resorts which were so busy in the summer have a slightly rundown air, but the coast itself is a delight to walk.

The excellent Glasgow-Ayr rail service makes this walk an easy proposition at any time. Trains run twice every hour, even on Sundays. This walk starts at Irvine but it could just as easily be done in the opposite direction.

Although Irvine is one of Scotland's "New Towns", designated for commercial and residential growth, it has plenty of historical interest, and if you have time to spare it is well worth visiting the Glasgow Vennel, a street which has been completely restored to the way it looked when Robert Burns worked here as a flax-dresser between 1781 and 1784. *(See Irvine town trail)*

Mary, Queen of Scots visited Irvine in August 1563 and her visit is recalled every year in August with the Marymass, a week of festivities with a 'queen' being crowned as one of the highlights.

The walk starts from Irvine Station. From the Ayr platform, cross under the lines and continue straight ahead along Montgomery Street. You soon come to the Scottish Maritime Museum on the right, a fascinating place where visitors can see traditional maritime skills being practised and can pick up and handle many of the tools and equipment used by seamen past and present. A Clyde

Boats on display at the Scottish Maritime Museum, Irvine

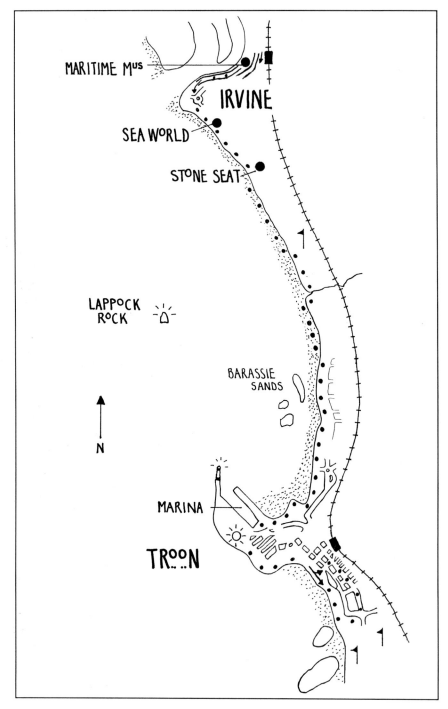

MARITIME MᵁˢS

IRVINE

SEA WORLD

STONE SEAT

LAPPᵒCK ROCK

N

BARASSIE SANDS

MARINA

TRᵒᵒN

Carved stone seat with Irvine in the background

puffer, the *Spartan*, and a tug, the *Garnock*, are on display too. The museum is open daily between April and the end of October, from 10am to 5pm.

Continue with the estuaries of the Irvine and Garnock Rivers on the right; there is always plenty of birdlife here. You soon pass The Ship Inn, which proudly proclaims itself as the oldest in Irvine, dating from 1597. It makes a curious contrast with the modern outline of the Magnum Leisure Centre just across the road.

About 200 yards past The Ship, go half-left across grass and continue to the beach. Offshore, you will see the outline of the hills on Arran — the famous "Sleeping warrior", reclining ready for the call to arms. This stretch of coast down to Ayr is one of the very many places associated with the legendary King Arthur and his Knights.

Pass the Sea World aquarium and cafe (open seven days) and continue on the path behind it. Troon is now visible in the distance. After a quarter of a mile, a short diversion leads up to a curious carved stone seat from which you can enjoy the seaward views before continuing the walk.

At a bend in the path below the stone seat, go through a gap in the fence and onto the beach. Walk southwards along this glorious stretch of sand, picking the firmest going. You may well see greyhounds being exercised here: it is believed the seawater is good for their leg muscles. Offshore is the light on Lappock Rock, and more often than not you will be accompanied by the calls of oystercatchers, a common bird along this stretch of coast.

In about a mile and a half, at the point where the dunes get lower, you can if you wish leave the beach and walk along the edge of Wester Gailes, one of many fine links golf courses on the Ayrshire coast. Troon is, of course, one of the courses used for the Open Championship, most recently in 1989 when the American golfer Mark Calcavecchia triumphed after an exciting three-man play-off.

You can get back onto the beach at any time. The constant surge of the sea can be an irresistable attraction, and beach walking a pure delight in surroundings like this where you can wander along at your own pace.

Soon enough the houses at Barassie (which has its own station) are reached. The wide stretch of grass between the houses and the beach gives excellent walking. Cross a burn by a footbridge near the road and continue past a putting green, to skirt a small boatyard on its seaward side. Now head gradually up to the road and join it for a short while, leaving it again at a car park to walk round Pan Rocks picnic area.

Where the path ends keep by the fence until, opposite the Anchorage Inn, you walk up to the road again, then go right across grass to reach Troon Marina, always full of interest with the many colourfully decked-out yachts.

From the Marina, cross the road and walk down Kennedy Road. At its end take the path opposite leading up to the viewfinder erected by Troon Community Council in 1983. It shows you that the prominent rock of Ailsa Craig, dead ahead, is 26 miles away, and points out many other features of interest. The name Troon, by the way, comes from a very old word for a headland. You find it (as Trwyn) at a number of places in Wales.

Return to the road and walk south along it, with the sea on your right, passing an attractively laid-out garden. Continue past a large sandstone church and the red-brick council offices on your left. The latter contain a tourist information centre which has lots of interesting leaflets and other material.

Turn left up St Meddans Road to its end to reach the attractive Troon Station — happily retained and not replaced by a modern shelter as so many have been. The ride all along this line is a delight. If you wish, the walk can easily be extended by a mile or so by continuing along the promenade to the south end of

Troon Marina, always busy with boats

Golfers on the 6th green at Wester Gailes

Troon to see the famous golf course before returning to the station.

From here you can also see Prestwick Airport, started as a venture in 1935 by the Duke of Hamilton and Group Captain MacIntyre, who in 1933 were the first men to fly over Mount Everest. Prestwick's fog-free record won it the licence as Scotland's only airport handling transatlantic traffic, a distinction it has now lost with the adoption of an "open skies" policy.

The Ayrshire coast gives enjoyable walking at all times of the year. The weather cannot be guaranteed, of course, and it is as well to go prepared.❑

Burns trail

This trail visits several sites connected with Scotland's most famous poet plus the 100-acre woodland setting of Rozelle Park. (Approx. 2¹⁄₂ miles walking plus return)

Burns cottage

AYR is an attractive, bustling town, reflecting the relative prosperity of the area. Its role as a holiday resort has diminished but the electrification in 1986 of the railway route from Glasgow has increased its attractiveness as a dormitory town, in common with Prestwick and Troon.

There is much of historical significance in the town itself but its best-known attraction is probably Burns Cottage at Alloway, in the vicinity of which are several other places of interest. Alloway is on a bus route from Ayr; it is up to the individual to decide how much use is made of this facility. If walking from Ayr station, cross the road and walk past the 1881 statue of Robert Burns

and turn left into Carrick Road. After half a mile, bear right into Monument Road and the entrance to Rozelle Park is reached after a further mile.

The park consists of 100 acres of woodland, gifted to Ayr in 1968, and includes Rozelle House, built in the 1750s by Robert Hamilton, who made his fortune in the Caribbean. It is now a restaurant and coffee shop. The house's former stables and servants' block are the location of the Maclaurin art gallery, which operates a programme of temporary exhibitions, covering fine art, sculpture, photography and crafts. The park

Right: Old Alloway Kirk with headstone to Burns' parents in the foreground

92

is well-known for rare trees, including American redwood and Lebanon cedar, and can be wandered through at will.

About half-a-mile beyond Rozelle is Burns Cottage, the "auld clay biggin" built by William Burnes, father of the poet Robert Burns. (His children dropped the "e".) Here Robert was born in 1759 and spent his early years. It appears to have become a mecca for Burns followers remarkably quickly, the first recorded Burns Supper being held at Alloway in 1801 by friends of the poet. They established the practice of regular gatherings at the cottage, which had become an ale house. The thatched structure is now a museum and shrine to the poet and attracts thousands of visitors each year. It chronicles his life of hardship in farming, his many amorous encounters and his rise as a poet, becoming the darling of fashionable Edinburgh society.

His first love (after the lassies, of course) was music and he was responsible for rescuing some 350 traditional folk songs, often adapting them and writing new words. He died in Dumfries in 1796, at the age of 37, due to heart disease brought on by rheumatic fever as a child.

Beyond the cottage is the Land o' Burns Centre, built on the former Alloway station goods yard, which has an exhibition area and audio-visual display on the life and times of the bard. Near to this are the Burns Monument, dating from 1823, Auld Brig o' Doon and Alloway Kirk.

In the monument gardens are two life-size statues of Burns characters Tam o' Shanter and Souter Johnny, carved by the Tarbolton stonemason James Thom, who became some-

Right: Burns monument

Carved headstone in old Alloway Kirk

The walking distance from Ayr station to Brig o' Doon is over 2$\frac{1}{2}$ miles. Return by the same route or by bus. ❑

thing of a cult figure as a result, and who produced almost 40 subsequent versions of the pair. The model for Tam is believed to be William Brown of Stair, but controversy exists over the original "Johnny".

Both the bridge and the church figure in Burns' narrative work *Tam O'Shanter.*

...Kirk-Alloway was drawing nigh,
Where ghaists and houlets nightly cry...

So runs the poem. Through the windows of the ruined church an inebriated Tam saw the witches and warlocks dancing. They spotted him and pursued him over the single-arch bridge. William Burnes is buried in Alloway Kirk, his headstone, replacing one broken by souvenir hunters, containing an epitaph by the bard. Burns' mother is buried in East Lothian. The church contains a sarcophagus and mort safes — iron grilles to prevent grave robbing.

In the churchyard are some superb examples of carved gravestones and a distinctive headstone in the shape of a tree trunk, marking the grave of a gamekeeper on Rozelle Estate.

Culzean Park

Splendid walk through Scotland's first country park which takes in woodland, cliff tops and several of the park's main features. (Around four miles, although detours can be made at will)

CULZEAN Castle is one of the most-visited attractions in Scotland, located 12 miles south of Ayr on a cliff-top overlooking the Firth of Clyde. It is not directly accessible by rail; take a bus from Ayr or Girvan. Culzean (pronounced Culain) was home to the Earls of Cassillis, senior branch of the Kennedy family, until gifted to the National Trust for Scotland in 1945. It is renowned for its Adam interiors, magnificent gardens and its country park.

The 10th Earl commissioned Robert Adam to completely remodel the house in 1777. Adam not only designed the building; he also took responsibility for the interior decoration, including furniture and fittings. The oval staircase and the round drawing room leading off it, with its breathtaking view across the Firth to Kintyre and Arran, are particularly of note. The National Trust has faithfully restored the house's Adam

Below: Culzean Castle with the Dolphin House and Round House on the beach below

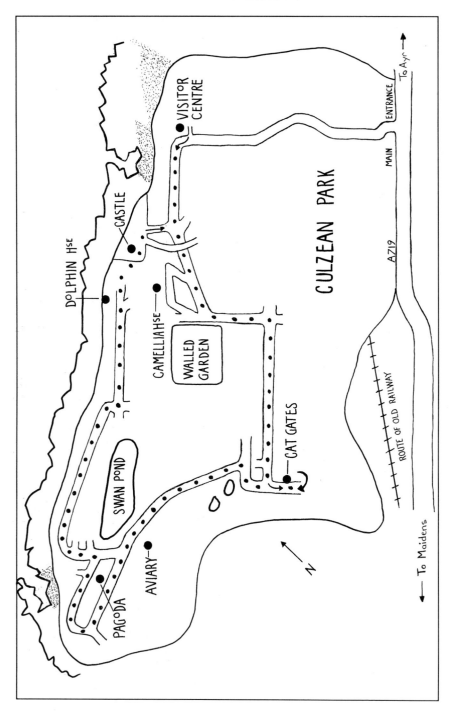

plasterwork and colour schemes, complementing the armour, furniture and paintings. Prominent among the portraits is Napoleon, with whom the Kennedy family appear to have had a minor obsession.

After the Second World War, the top flat was given to General Dwight D Eisenhower for his lifetime use, as a token of gratitude for his role as Allied Supreme Commander. He stayed in it several times, including once when he was US President. Today the Eisenhower Flat is let out to important visitors.

Robert Adam also designed the home farm, an Italiante range of buildings set around a courtyard entered by an arched gateway. These now form a visitor centre and include an exhibition covering the history of the property, as well as agriculture in Ayrshire. Culzean was Scotland's first country park, established in 1969; a move which was the turning point for the house and estate. The NTS had accepted Culzean in 1945 without an endowment (although an appeal at the time raised the remarkable sum of £20,000) and its upkeep was proving a ruinous drain on finances.

Now the house and park attract in excess of 300,000 visitors every year, many of them coming merely to wander the grounds, in which there are several miles of clearly defined paths through mixed woodland, formal gardens and along cliffs. The estate contains many 19th century additions such as the gas house, which used coal landed on the nearby shore to provide light, and the powder house, built in 1880 to store gunpowder for the time gun, fired every morning at eight. Many of these features are falling into disrepair, such as the pagoda which is now a roofless ruin. A debate continues as to their fate.

The route of the former Maidens and Dunure light railway runs close to the country park boundaries. Glenside, the station for the castle, was located on what is now a camping site near the main entrance. This alternative route between Ayr and Girvan was opened in 1905, chiefly to serve the Glasgow and South Western Railway's large hotel and golf course at Turnberry. Passenger services between Ayr and Turnberry ceased in the early 1930s; those between Girvan and Turnberry did not restart after World War Two. Freight, mostly potato traffic, kept the entire line open until 1955. The northern section was reopened to passengers from Alloway Junction to Heads of Ayr following the establishment of a Butlin's holiday camp, and trains, including through workings to such destinations as Edinburgh, ran for about 20 years until the end of the 1968 season.

There are several walks through the country park, from gentle strolls to a strenuous scramble up a stream bed. This suggested route takes in woodland and cliff tops and includes several of the main features.

Starting from the visitor centre, follow the path towards the castle and continue under the viaduct onto the main tarmac road. Visible on the right is the Camellia House, which may have been designed as an orangery and awaits restoration, when funds are available. It is easy to make a slight detour to view it more closely. Continue along the road, bearing left at the walled garden and into woodland. Walk through the woods, swinging right at a crossroads and a T-junction is eventually reached. Going left quickly leads to the Cat Gates, situated on one of the original driveways. The two lodge cottages have been demolished.

Retrace your steps to the T-junction and go straight on, then left alongside ponds to regain the tarmac road. Cross it to a path leading to the man-made Swan Pond, beside which is an aviary and tearoom. Go round by the left-hand side of the pond and a path bears off to the left which passes the pagoda, an-

Viaduct approach to the castle

other ruin. Built in 1860, the lower part housed swans and was an aviary and the upper section, a gazebo, was a tea-house. This circular path leads to the viewpoint of Barwhin Hill. It also gives access to the beach, which stretches towards Maidens.

Back at the Swan Pond, turn sharp left and up the track to the cliff tops and make your way through the trees, pausing to admire the seaward views and the prospect of the castle in its lofty position. On the beach below the castle are grouped together the Dolphin House, formerly a laundry and now a private residence, a ruined bathhouse, and a curious round stone building which was a changing room for bathers. Further along is a wooden boathouse; at one time the estate maintained its own rescue boat.

Walk diagonally across parkland and a gate on the other side leads to the formal gardens of the Fountain Court from which paths lead back to the visi-

tor centre, up to the castle or to the main park road. The distance is around four miles but detours can be made at whim; distances between features in the surprisingly compact country park are not great.

Check the bus service before starting out as it can be somewhat restricted. ❏

Left: Visitor centre at Culzean country park

101

Town trails

The canal at Coatbridge

Short walks around some of Strathclyde's principal towns, each of which, in one way or another, has played a major role in the region's history.

Lanark

*The busy market town of Lanark offers
scope for many walks of varying nature.
Here are three of them. The first takes in
the magnificent World Heritage Centre
at New Lanark and the town trail recalls
the area's medieval past with a walk
around historic sites and buildings.*

LANARK is situated at the end of a rail branch from the West Coast Main Line, served by suburban electrics running on Argyle Line routes. To begin the walk to New Lanark and the Falls of Clyde turn left into Ladyacre Road on leaving the station then cross into Albany Drive and turn left into Braxfield Road. You will see on your right two similar buildings, originally New Lanark gatehouses. Do not take the road between them but continue straight on down a lane, turning right into another track. This becomes pleasantly wooded, with the Ponclair Burn on the left. Ignore a flight

of stone steps encountered on the right and continue until you emerge at New Lanark, at the end of Caithness Row. You may find it remarkable that anything so complex could be so well hidden on your route down!

New Lanark, now designated a World Heritage Centre, is simply magnificent, combining industrial archaeology, social history and modern living. It was begun around 1785 as a village centred round a cotton mill powered by the Falls of Clyde. Its backers were Richard Arkwright, inventor of a water-powered spinning machine, and David Dale,

New Lanark in the Clyde Valley

a Glasgow linen merchant. By 1799, it was the largest cotton mill in Scotland, employing 2,000 people under what, for the time, were excellent conditions of housing and education, thanks to Dale's philanthropic approach. This was reinforced when Dale's daughter Caroline married Robert Owen, the social reformer who gained an international reputation for his work at New Lanark, where he built a large school and the quaintly-named Institute for the Formation of Character. He was also responsible for the Counting House at the end of Caithness Row, from which the whole village could be surveyed. Caithness Row is thought to have been so named because of the would-be emigrants from the Highlands who left for the New World but ended up in New Lanark, due to their ship being stormbound.

The mills worked until 1968, producing cotton threads and canvas. Since then a housing association and conservation trust have restored and renovated much of the village. Caithness Row, for instance, which once housed 300 Highlanders, is now 16 modern flats. There is a visitor centre, presenting a ten-minute view of village life, seen through the eyes of a ten-year-old mill girl. A walk round the village is a rewarding experience.

The Scottish Wildlife Trust has taken over the former dyeworks to tell the story of the Falls of Clyde, by means of an audio-visual display and exhibitions. The river at this point is a favourite place for dippers. The woods along the Clyde are owned by the Trust and managed as the Falls of Clyde Nature Reserve. Follow the riverbank path past the smallest of the three waterfalls, the Dundaff Linn, till you arrive at Bonnington Power Station, into which the main flow of water is directed in order to generate electricity. Opened in 1927, this was the first public hydro-electric scheme in Scotland. At certain pre-advertised times of year the power station closes for maintenance and full flow is restored to the falls.

The next falls, Corra Linn, mark the start of the most spectacular section of the gorge. A summer house, built in 1708 by Sir James Carmichael, overlooks the Linn. It once contained mirrors to reflect the scene, avoiding the need for those suffering from vertigo to look directly at the falls. The first viewing platform is 90 feet above the river. Take the second flight of steps and continue for half a mile to Bonnington Linn, where the River Clyde enters the Clyde Gorge and a series of rapids descend to Corra Linn.

Retrace your steps to the power station and return to New Lanark by the hill path. At the church in the main street take the steep and obviously old path up the hill (not the modern path to the car park), turning right at the top till the gatehouses previously referred to are reached, then return to Lanark station by the original route. *Total distance about five miles.*

Lanark Loch

An alternative walk follows Ladyacre Road to its junction with Hyndford Road, at which is situated Lanark Market.

Crossing the road gives a good view of the market and its octagonal auction rings. While you are there, take a look at the ruins of the Church of St Kentigern, dating from the 15th Century. Continue along Hyndford Road, past the convalescent homes of Lady Hozier House and Crosslaw Home, until the entrance to Lanark Loch car park is reached on the left, next to the embankment of the Caledonian Railway's line to Muirkirk, where an end-on connection was made with the Glasgow and South Western. From the car park, bear right round

Corra Linn, Falls of Clyde

by the loch and over the hill to Lanark Moor car park, at the racecourse. Bearing left, walk along the racecourse edge, through an opening in the fence (after about a quarter of a mile) and continue through pine woods to the golf course. At the far side of the course the track divides. Take the left hand route (which does not cross the railway line) and return past the clubhouse to Lanark Loch. This is artificial, built in the 1830s to augment the town's water supply. Today its use is solely leisure and recreational. Return along Hyndford Road to Home Street then left into Whitelees Road and back to the station. *(Distance four miles)*

Town trail

Turn left outside the station and cross to St Mary's Church Close, whose iron gates lead to a 19th century convent with an ornate chapel. St Mary's RC Church was badly damaged by fire in 1902 and the tall slender steeple is a replacement. The building on the other side of the wall next to the steeple base was St Mary's Hospital and is now used by the District Council. It is worthwhile walking round the back of the church for the views south and west. Return to the gates and turn left, making your way towards High Street, the town's main thoroughfare, along which the view westwards ends neatly with St Nicholas Church. Continuity of the building lines was achieved by the town council which, in the 18th century, paid proprietors to conform.

A number of closes gave access from the High Street to the areas to the north. At the west end of the street turn right into one of the best-surviving examples, Shirley's Close, named after a Doctor Shirley. Turn left into the North Vennel (the word vennel is of French origin and meant lane) and right into Greenside Lane, with its mixture of architecture old and new, leading to the top of Hope Street. This was once the administrative centre of the town and has some fine

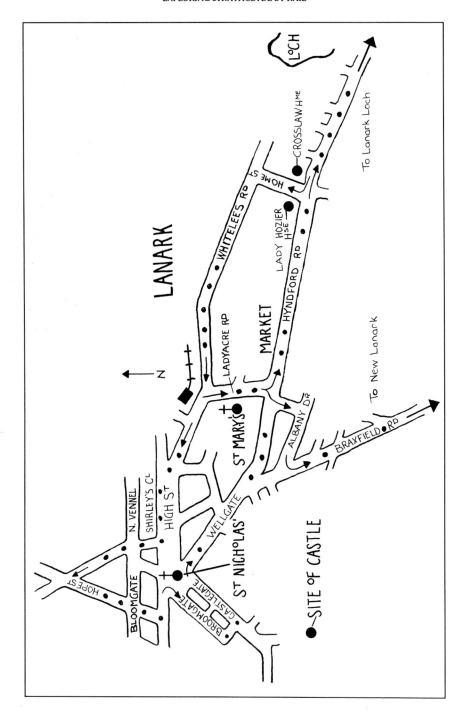

buildings. The first is the Episcopal Christ Church, from 1858, at the corner of Greenside Lane. The street also contains the Council Registrar's Office, which began life as a church (and was once a hosiery factory) and whose neo-Georgian façade is worthy of study, as is the detailed doorway; Lanark Sheriff Court and the former Council Chambers alongside; the Church of St Kentigern with its 138 foot spire; and the Lindsay Institute, a public library gifted to the town by local benefactor Charles Lindsay.

Before turning left from Hope Street into Bloomgate, take a look at the YMCA halls and Cairns Church opposite, the circular turret and crow-stepped gable of one contrasting with the buttressed façade and octagonal tower of the other. In Bloomgate, a plaque on the Clydesdale Hotel records patronage by Dorothy and William Wordsworth and Samuel Taylor Coleridge in 1803. Charles Dickens was also a visitor to this coaching inn, which stands on the site of a Greyfriars Monastery. Swing right at The Cross, in front of St Nicholas Church, whose tower houses what is reputedly Europe's oldest bell, although it has been recast several times. It sounded the medieval curfew and a plaque on the north side of the tower reads: "I did for thrice three cent'ries hing, and unto Lanark city ring." Above the main door is a statue of Sir William Wallace, whose house was nearby and whose fight to free Scotland from Edward I of England began in Lanark. Proceed along the south side of St Nicholas and down Broomgate. Tucked in on the left, next to the ironmonger's, is Hyndford House with its crow-stepped gables, one of the oldest buildings in the town. The Broomgate Institute, now converted into flats, was built in 1838 as a school for the poor. At the foot of the street, a bowling green occupies the site of Lanark Castle, hence the name Castlegate, the oldest street

and centre of the medieval town. Walk back towards the town centre, encountering on the way No 30 Castlegate, on which a plaque proclaims this to be the site of Castlegate Port. Don't miss the statue of a dog on the roof of number 15, allegedly placed there by a man who suspected a woman living in the street of poisoning his dog, the idea being that this would serve as a permanent reminder of her crime.

At the end of Castlegate, turn right into Wellgate, with the Old Tolbooth at the corner of Wellgate and High Street, and proceed eastward along Wellgate, which takes its name from the town well. Look along to the right at Wellgatehead and you will see a white toll house. Continue to Hyndford Road, past what is now an annexe to Lanark Grammar, located in Albany Drive behind, and at the corner of Ladyacre Road, turn left and return to the station. *Distance $1^3/_4$ miles.* ❑

Bowling

An interesting walk, part of which follows the Glasgow-Loch Lomond cycleway, around what used to be the heart of the area's transport network. (2½ miles)

NOT many places can boast of having been the meeting point of two railway routes, a canal, a river and a main road. This claim can, however, be made by Bowling. Today, one of the rail routes has gone; the canal is disused; the river is quiet and the main road by-passes the village. However, sufficient remains to give an inkling of days past. In the 1850s, Bowling was a major transport interchange and goods and passengers brought by the canal were taken by rail to Dumbarton and Balloch and then by steamer up Loch Lomond.

On leaving Bowling station, take some steps on the other side of the main road and go through trees to gain access to the Glasgow to Loch Lomond cycle route where it runs through an old railway tunnel. This carried the line under what was the drive to Auchentorlie House, before, of course, the A82 got in the way. The eastern portal of the tunnel is more ornate than its western counterpart and carries the date 1895. The author is grateful to the descriptive leaflet produced in connection with the Glasgow-Loch Lomond cycleway for the information that, because the tunnel runs east-west, there are interesting sunrise and sunset effects. It seems that during the middle of September and the last week of March between 6.30 and 7.30, the sun sets to shine directly into the tunnel. The leaflet goes on: "The most spectacular effect, however, is the sunrise occurring between 7.30 and 8.00 in the last week of September/first week of October and the middle weeks of March. Provided the weather is good, the sun shines straight up the cutting from the old station, through the tunnel, and out the other side to strike the rock face beyond."

Head east along the cycleway, past the remains of the other Bowling station, which closed in 1951 — obviously the degree of duplication was too much even for this over-endowed area. Just before the old rail bridge over the A814, come off through the park and cross over to another road which leads down to the canal. (Note the wartime relic of an Anderson shelter behind the wooden

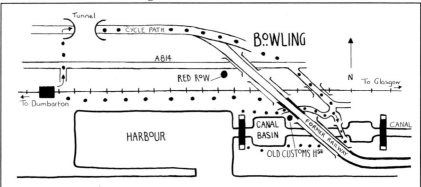

Canal Basin, Bowling with former customs house and Lanarkshire and Dumbartonshire Railway opening bridge in background

shop.) At this point the Lanarkshire and Dumbartonshire Railway of 1896 crossed the Forth and Clyde Canal, the Helensburgh line and the Dumbarton road in quick succession. A massive swing bridge was built over the canal and a new lock and inner basin provided. The bridge was controlled by a signalbox which straddled the tracks at the western end of the steelwork.

Although this section of the Lanarkshire and Dumbartonshire closed in 1964, its three bridges are still in place. If you stand on the road bridge over the present electrified route, facing towards the river, the signalbox would have been directly ahead. The large building visible on the far bank is Erskine Hospital, a home for ex-servicemen. Look down to the right at the imaginative brickwork of the filled-in arches — not many

people went to that much trouble.

Walking across the small canal bridge and then under the old swing bridge leads to the outer canal basin. (It is possible to walk right round the basin in a clockwise circle, crossing the lock gates at the harbour end.) Some of the boats moored here are used as accommodation. The old custom house, a reminder of Bowling's former role, still stands on the north side of the basin. An unofficial path runs between the railway line and the harbour, by which it is possible to return to the railway station, if there are no objections to a bit of a scramble at the station end. Alternatively go back to the road and follow it to the station. Encountered on the way is the very unScottish three-storey brick tenement called, appropriately, Red Row and dating from 1894. ❑

Dumbarton

A walk around sites connected with the historic town's maritime and military past. (Approx. two miles)

DUMBARTON Central has survived the march of progress, at least at platform level where the brick buildings and steel-framed awnings remain, although possibly not for much longer: the buildings are out of use and at the time of writing a station improvement scheme was being promised. The entrance has been modernised but the original ticket-issuing windows are discernible. It is served by both electric and West Highland Line trains and was formerly a Dumbarton and Balloch Joint Line station. There used to be a memorial on the east gable of one of the station buildings to commemorate employees of the Line who died in the Great War.

On leaving the station, cross the road and turn right. Continue past the library and take the underpass, bearing left at the other side. Walk alongside the main road, passing the remains of Dumbarton prison, which was demolished in 1973 to make way for the present road, having long ceased to be a jail. This relatively recent road is then crossed by a railway line, which once served the large whisky blending and bottling plant on the right. It had been out of use for some time before the track north of the main road was lifted in the late 1980s, during construction of a retail development.

The building housing the Denny ship model experiment tank, the oldest surviving example of its kind in the world, is on the right. Built in 1882-83, it was used, for 100 years, on a commercial basis to test ships' hulls and propellers, before becoming part of the Irvine-based Scottish Maritime Museum. Scale model hulls, fashioned in wood or wax, were tested in the 330 foot long tank, which was equipped with an electric carriage and wavemaker. This, of course, was before computer-aided design! As well as the tank, visitors can see the model-making workshops and the drawing office, where the records list many famous nautical names. *Enquiries about opening times should be made to 0389 63444.*

As recently as late 1989, a find of enormous historical significance was made in one of the test facility's sheds — a model hull of the Q3, the 1960s Cunard liner which was never built. The contract had gone not to John Brown's of Clydebank, builders of the two Queens, but to a consortium of Vickers Armstrong and Swan Hunter on Tyneside. Only tank testing was tendered to John Brown's; the model presumably ended up at Dumbarton and was forgotten about. It must be one of the few surviving links with the Q3, which was abandoned in favour of a smaller, more economical alternative — the *Queen Elizabeth 2*. Following restoration to Cunard colours in 1990, the model went on show in Glasgow.

On leaving the test tank building, walk along the main road past the supermarket and turn right into Leven Street. The route passes the former Denny's shipyard, and streets of what were superior workers' houses dating from the 1880s. A right turn into Castle Road leads to Dumbarton Castle.

Right: Glass canopy of Dumbarton station

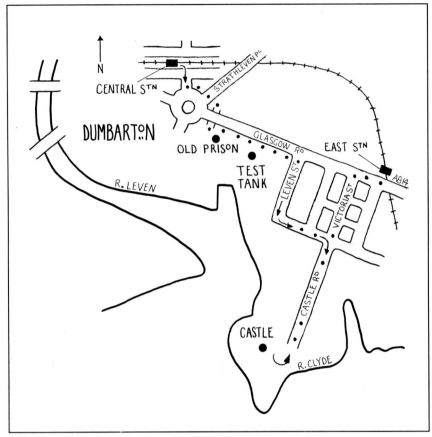

Dumbarton Rock, at the confluence of the Rivers Clyde and Leven, is the oldest recorded stronghold site in Britain. From at least the 5th century AD to 1018, it was the centre of the independent kingdom of Strathclyde. The name Dumbarton comes from Dun Breatann, meaning Fortress of the Britons. Its strategic significance lay in its proximity to what was the lowest crossing point of the River Clyde, until it was artificially deepened. Like Edinburgh and Stirling, Dumbarton was a royal castle and had close links with Mary, Queen of Scots. Thereafter it became a coastal battery and a base for keeping an eye on troublesome Jacobites, being one of four Scots castles to remain fortified after the Union of the Parliaments in 1707.

Most of what is to be seen today dates from the 17th and 18th centuries and is attributed to General Wade, of road-making fame, and William Skinner, who was responsible for the magnificent Fort George, near Inverness. The Governor's House and the V-shaped King George's Battery, with its pepper-pot sentry box, date from 1735. A similar sentry box exists on the east curtain wall. Both are the work of Captain John Romer, Wade's engineer, and although in keeping with traditionally Scottish corbelled turrets, are in fact of continental inspiration.

Skinner was responsible for the barrel-vaulted powder magazine on The Beak, the eastern lower summit. The fort was abandoned by 1865 but this part of the rock saw military occupation as comparatively recently as the Second World War, when it was the location of an anti-aircraft battery, of which no trace survives.

Retrace your steps along Castle Road, continue into Victoria Street and turn right along the main Glasgow road.

Dumbarton East station is about 100 yards away. Until 1984 it had a platform building in the style of Dumbarton Central, although it was originally a Lanarkshire and Dumbartonshire Railway station.

Alternatively, a return can be made to Dumbarton Central. By either route, the walking distance is around two miles. ❏

Dumbarton castle

113

Paisley

*A walk around the famous
textile town which features
the only surviving stretch
of the Glasgow-Ardrossan
canal. (About three miles)*

PAISLEY, Scotland's biggest town, was built on textiles, reflected by street names such as Gauze, Silk and Cotton. Its weavers recreated the patterned shawls of Kashmir, at a fraction of the cost of the Indian originals, and gave the English language a new adjective — Paisley — referring to the pattern style. Thread-makers such as Coats dominated the market, and, at the same time, the town. In 1826 James Coats founded his Ferguslie Mills, which grew to be an impressive complex of simply magnificent industrial buildings, which by the spring of 1990 were in various stages of demolition and dereliction. Through the site runs the only surviving stretch of the Glasgow, Paisley and Ardrossan Canal, complete with overbridges.

Paisley's chief station is Gilmour Street, opened in the 1840s by the Glasgow and Paisley Joint Railway. The two-storey main building is original, although doubtless it was seen to better advantage when its surroundings were less obtrusive. The four-platform station stands on arches and is served by Ayrshire and Wemyss Bay/Gourock electric trains.

The walk starts from the station and continues along Gilmour Street to The Cross and right into High Street. Pause for a moment to admire the imposing war memorial, unusual in that the sculpture surmounting it includes the figure of a knight. The way in which the World War One soldiers succeed in conveying an impression of weariness is a tribute to the sculptor's art. Note also the former tram wire fixture on the wall of the building at the corner of Moss Street and High Street, a reminder of the transport of the past. The last Paisley trams ran in May 1957, by which time the operators were Glasgow Corporation Transport. The tram depot was at Elderslie, near the railway junction of the Canal Line and the Joint Line. Moss Street corner was also the site, until 1870, of the Tolbooth and steeple, which served as municipal buildings, courthouse and jail.

Walk westwards along High Street to No 22 on the right, the site of the town house of the Semples, an important Renfrewshire family whose country estate of Castle Semple gives its name to the leisure park at Lochwinnoch. An armorial panel can be seen high on the façade of the present building.

Further along on the right is the steep Church Hill, which leads to the High Church, whose spire dominates the Paisley skyline. As you pause for breath half-way up, take a look at the Middle Church on the right, which dates from around 1780. After its congregation amalgamated with that of another church in 1975, it became a centre for the homeless. (A striking feature of walking round central Paisley is the number of churches or former churches one encounters.) Past the High Church, our route swings left into Oakshaw Street, with views northwards across Paisley to Glasgow Airport and beyond, to reach Hutcheson's Charity School, on the corner of Oakshaw Street and Orr Street.

Right: Church Hill, Paisley

114

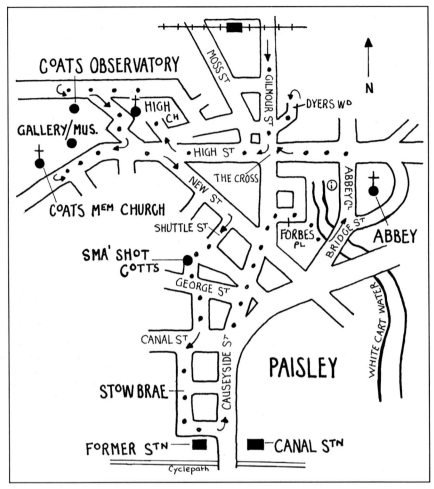

It was established by Margaret Hutcheson to provide impoverished children with a basic education, which it did until 1889 when its endowments were transferred towards the John Neilson Institute, whose original building is 200 yards to the west.

In the same direction is Coats Observatory, financed by Thomas Coats of the thread-making family. It was one of the first buildings planned with the disabled in mind, for Thomas Coats was confined to a wheelchair. Sadly, he died in 1883 without seeing his observatory opened. In 1963 it passed from the Philosophical Institution to Paisley Town Council, which carried out much-needed repairs, and in 1975 to Renfrew District Council, which has upgraded the building and equipment. It is now a major seismic station, as well as being active in astronomy and weather reporting and recording.

Return to Hutcheson's School and turn down Orr Street, with its high walls, to Orr Square, which in the Middle Ages marked the westernmost limit of Paisley. This was the site of the town's first hospital, which was more of an alms-house. The present buildings, a pair of houses and Orr Square Church and hall, occupied the site early last century. The church and its hall are worthy of comparison, as much for their points of difference as points of similarity. The hall, for instance, has a more elaborate doorway than the church.

Proceed down Orr Square back to High Street, where a right turn is required to visit the art gallery and museum, a feature of which is a display of Paisley shawls. About 100 yards further on is the impressive Coats Memorial Church. Retrace your steps to New Street, on the left of which is the Bull Inn, which retains its Art Nouveau interior and fittings. Built in 1901 it was designed by local architect W P McLellan, whose style was said to have similarities to that of Charles Rennie Mackintosh. The exterior of the Bull Inn is indeed reminiscent of early Mackintosh, if somewhat subdued.

The next stop is at the corner of New Street and Shuttle Street. On the left is the Laigh Kirk (or Low Church) built in 1738 as overspill accommodation for the Abbey. Principal John Witherspoon of Princeton University, the only clergyman to sign the American Declaration of Independence, was minister here before leaving for the New World in 1768. (A memorial to him can be found in Paisley Abbey.) A round plaque on the side records the renovations carried out by the Evangelical Union in 1873. Closed in 1980, it is now an arts centre.

Across the road in Shuttle Street, the Paisley College lecture hall is housed in what was the Free Gaelic Church, its simple lines reflecting the restricted finances of the breakaway congregation of Highland weaving stock who set it up following the Disruption of 1843. The original building of 1793 still stands in Oakshaw Street, an earlier part of this walk.

Walking up Shuttle Street and bearing right leads to Sma' Shot Cottages in George Place, restored and furnished millworkers' housing in typical Scottish style, with a rear iron staircase. *Opening times are restricted so it is best to check with the Paisley Historical Society (041 812 2153/889 0530).*

Cross George Street into Wardour Street and continue over Canal Street into Stow Brae, where a restaurant and bar have been fashioned out of the original 1885 Paisley Canal station, closed along with the rest of the Glasgow-Kilmacolm route in January 1983. The Glasgow-Irvine cycle path now occupies part of the trackbed, including the stretch through Paisley Canal. The station's main offices were in a now-demolished wooden building on the Causeyside Street overbridge, on the east side of which is located the present Canal station, built when the line was reopened to passengers in 1990, it having been realised too late that the Glasgow to Paisley Canal section should not have been a casualty of the Kilmacolm line demise. Further reinstatement beyond Paisley Canal is not possible, as houses have been built across the trackbed.

Facing the town centre, walk along Causeyside Street to the striking Russell Institute on the corner of New Street. Donated to the burgh in 1927 by Miss Agnes Russell in memory of her two lawyer brothers, it was to be used for the welfare of mothers and children and is still a clinic. It is built of reinforced concrete, faced with stone, and is the work of local architects.

Crossing over to Forbes Place on the right brings us down a street of 19th century shawl warehouses, in which were finished and displayed the shawls produced by the weavers, who worked from home. Bear right alongside the White Cart Water to the Abbey Bridge, a product of local firm Hanna, Donald

and Wilson (who also made such items as railway footbridges). Erected in 1879, it was widened in 1933. Note the ornamental railings on the abbey side of the river, which have a Gothic tracery design.

On the south side of the Abbey stands the Place (Palace) of Paisley, monastic buildings which, following the Reformation, became a mansion. The Place had deteriorated badly by 1903 when the Kirk Session bought it back and many years of work culminated in the creation of the Abbey Manse in the 1950s.

The abbey itself began as a Cluniac priory founded about 1163 and replacing a Celtic monastery dedicated to Saint Mirin. Its origins are linked to the High Stewards of Scotland, from whom the Royal Stewart line extends, and in 1888 Queen Victoria presented the Abbey with a marble tombstone, in memory of her Stewart ancestors. Much of the church originates in 15th century reconstruction, being of cross plan with a long choir, aisled nave and a tower over the crossing. For 300 years, until the late 19th century, the choir and tower were in ruins with only the nave in use as the parish church (hence the need for the Laigh Kirk previously referred to). A feature of the reconstruction is the Great East window, designed by Douglas Strachan.

The walk continues past the statue of weaver-poet, Robert Tannahill, and alongside the Town Hall in Gauze Street and right into Gilmour Street. Before returning to the railway station, divert down Dyers Wynd on the right which was the scene of the Glen Cinema tragedy on December 31, 1929, when smoke at a New Year matinee started a panic in which 70 children died. A memorial in Hawkhead Cemetery lists their names.

Coats Mills and the old canal

Rail and canal history can be combined in Paisley with a walk to the last remaining stretch of the Paisley, Johnstone and Ardrossan Canal. The route follows the former rail line which superseded the canal, which in turn is now part of the Glasgow to Irvine cyclepath. However, the railway did deviate from the canal at certain points.

Begin at the modern Paisley Canal station, opened on July 27, 1990 walking through the underpass and past the original station building. The cyclepath goes behind houses built on the track bed then picks up the line of the original railway, which is mostly in cutting. Signal cable brackets can still be seen on the walls.

After almost a mile, a modern concrete overbridge comes into view. Veer off left just before this, turning right into Craw Road and crossing the bridge and then Maxwellton Street, the main road. Facing you is the site of James Coats' Ferguslie Mills, through which the canal runs on the right. It can be seen with a bit of peering through undergrowth but, at the time of writing, there was no official public access at this point and the huge mill complex, was, sadly, in varying stages of demolition.

The wonderfully-ornate building to the right of the canal dates from 1887 and was a school set up by Coats. It lies on Maxwellton Street and has been converted into a night club.

Return by the cyclepath, making the total walking distance about two miles. ❑

Left: Coats Observatory

119

Coatbridge

*A walk around one of the old
industrial heartlands of the area
plus a visit to a country park*

Entrance to Summerlee heritage museum

IF *one* town can claim to have been at the centre of the industrial and transport revolutions in Scotland, it has to be Coatbridge. The Monkland Canal ran through the town; it was close to the earliest Scottish railways and on the route of the first trunk line.

Coatbridge was built on iron — the Monklands area was rich in blackband ironstone and coal and, following the invention by James Beaumont Neilson of the hot blast method of smelting iron ore in 1828, the place grew from a village into a major town, whose night skies were permanently lit by the glow of the blast furnaces. A myriad of railway lines served the pits and ironworks, and at one point there were 280 miles of running lines within a seven-mile radius of Coatbridge.

It goes without saying that a skeleton remains where once there was a healthy body of industry. What is left of the Monkland Canal can still be traced in the town centre; the former Caledonian Railway main line to the north still functions and electric trains to and from Airdrie serve the town. Railway freight business is represented by the container depot at Gartsherrie and traffic generated by Mossend yard. The traditional iron industry has survived, to an extent.

It is no surprise that an area so steeped in industrial archaeology boasts an excellent heritage museum. Summerlee, on the site of an 1830s ironworks, proudly claims to be Scotland's noisiest museum. With its belt-driven machinery operating in recreated workshops, steam cranes, railway locomotives and displays of everyday life, it is a working tribute to 200 years of industrial and social history, and the struggle for decent housing, proper sanitation and a living wage.

The original ironworks, demolished in the 1920s, have been excavated and the Monkland Canal, which served it, has been restored. The end wall of the huge exhibition hall is entirely of glass, giving a superb view of the canal and the town. At the entrance to the 25-acre site, a row of 19th century cottages has been rebuilt, and it is even possible to ride on a tramcar.

The nearest station to Summerlee is Coatbridge Central, which has an electric train link to Motherwell. Coatbridge Sunnyside, on the suburban electric network through Glasgow Queen Street low level, may prove more convenient. To get to Summerlee from Coatbridge Central, turn left and go under the railway bridge, with the landscaped canal area on the opposite side of the road, then left at the former station building, now licensed premises, and continue to the heritage museum entrance. From Sunnyside, built by the North British Railway in 1888, turn left outside the station down Sunnyside Road, right at The Cross (where rail, canal and road traffic including tramcars once met) into West Canal Street and right at Coatbridge Central. *Total distance from Sunnyside is half-a-mile.*

In contrast, alighting at Blairhill station, the one before Coatbridge Sunnyside when heading from Glasgow, allows a walk to Drumpellier country park, a distance of $1^1/_2$ miles. (This can be reached after visiting Summerlee by retracing the route to Sunnyside station and boarding a westbound train.) Turn right outside the station, left at the roundabout into

Townhead Road and continue to the entrance.

Drumpellier Park was presented to the burgh of Coatbridge in 1919, no doubt offering the industrial workers a breath of fresh air, and was designated a country park in 1984. The lochs are natural, formed at the end of the Ice Age by retreating glaciers, which deposited uneven layers of boulder clay in ridges and hollows. The remains of the ridges, or drumlins, can be seen to the west of the park and the hollows filled with water to become Lochend and Woodend lochs. These are stocked with rainbow trout (fishing by permit only) and perch and pike are also present. In Lochend loch, the site of a crannog, an Iron Age dwelling built on an artificial island, is indicated by a buoy.

An excellent nature trail, marked by posts, takes a circular route from the visitor centre. It is named the Rovers' Nature Trail, to commemorate the success of the local football team, Albion Rovers, in winning the Scottish League Division Two Championship in the 1988-89 season. Allow at least an hour for the trail. *Enquiries about the park can be made on (0236) 22257.*

Return to Blairhill station by the same route. ❑

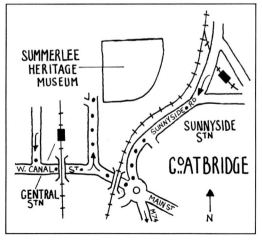

Part of the old canal in the heritage museum grounds

Former Coatbridge Central station building, now a restaurant

Summerlee main building

Hamilton

*In the heart of industrial Lanarkshire
lies a mixture of history and wide
open spaces, accessible by train
thanks to a complex electric network*

BEFORE doing the Hamilton town trail, take a ride on the Hamilton Circle — a rail route which begins and ends at Newton, a station whose surroundings encapture the industrial decline of the area. The circle can be gone round in either direction, depending on which service is used. Assuming anti-clockwise travel, the first station of interest is Blantyre, which, by turning right out of the station and following the road for half-a-mile, leads to the David Livingstone Centre. Livingstone, renowned as an African explorer and missionary, crossed the Kalahari Desert, discovered Lake Ngami and trekked to the mouth of the Zambesi River, discovering the Victoria Falls. He died in 1873 trying to find the source of the Nile, two years after his famous meeting with H M Stanley at

Ujiji. ("Doctor Livingstone, I presume.")

The focal point of the centre is the single-end (one-roomed tenement house) in which Livingstone was born in 1813. As well as the African connections, which are extensively dealt with, the centre is of significance in the field of industrial archaeology, as Livingstone worked from the age of ten as a piecer in the cotton mill established by David Dale of New Lanark fame, and there are displays on the impact of the industrial revolution. Before returning to the station, view the River Clyde from the footbridge erected in 1952, which leads to Bothwell.

The town trail begins at Hamilton Central station, turning right into Brandon Street and left down pedestrianised Quarry Street to the Old Cross. Bear left down Castle Street and cross the road at the roundabout, where Hamilton District Museum, the Regimental Museum of the Cameronians, and the entrance to Strathclyde Country Park are conveniently together. Walk through the park to the domed Hamilton Mausoleum, begun in 1841 by Alexander, the tenth Duke of Hamilton, whose flamboyant manner earned him the nickname of *Il Magnifico*, and who died before it was completed in 1857. This remarkable building, the stones of which dovetail into each other, virtually without mortar, was intended to be a family burial place with a chapel above. However, it was never used for worship, due to its remarkable echo...lasting 15 seconds! It remains as a monument to the efforts of the rich to perpetuate their memory and access is by guided tour only. *Telephone (0698) 66155 for details.*

Hamilton mausoleum

Strathclyde Park is worthy of a visit in its own right and is dealt with separately at the end of this section.

Return to the park entrance and the building on the right is the museum of the Cameronians (Scottish Rifles), located in the former Hamilton family riding stables. Mementoes, uniforms, medals, photographs and relics chart the history of the now disbanded regiment from 1689 to modern times. *Check with (0698) 428688 for opening details.*

Alongside is Hamilton District Museum, in what was a 17th century coaching inn. Here the London to Glasgow coach changed horses, relieving those which had been put on at Abington, in Lanarkshire. Incidentally, the fare from Hamilton to Carlisle was 17s 6d (87$\frac{1}{2}$p) outside the coach; 27s 6d (£1.37$\frac{1}{2}$p) inside. The museum has a strong transport theme, with emphasis on coaching and horse-haulage relics, but also including some historic cars, parts of a home-made aeroplane dating from the late 1930s and a World War Two bomb casing, cast in a Hamilton foundry, which may appear to be stretching the definition of transport a bit far! There are also changing displays and aspects of local life. Between its time as an inn and becoming a museum, the building served as an estate office.

Cross the road outside the museum into Portwell, continuing to Church Street, topped by the parish church. At the corner of Postgate is the Trades House, dating from 1816 and one of the few remaining links with old Hamilton. After crossing Cadzow Street, look right for a view of the council chambers then follow Cadzow Lane, to the left of the church gates, to the main road, to gain access to the church grounds in which there are two points of interest. On the east wall is the Heads Memorial, commemorating four Covenanters executed at Rullion Green, outside Edinburgh, after the Pentland Rising of 1666. The heads of the four were publicly displayed at Hamilton. In front of the church is the Netherton Cross, an early Christian relic which originally stood near Mote Hill (adjacent to what is now Strathclyde Park), which was the site of an early church. It was moved in 1926. The church itself is by William Adam and dates from 1734, with alterations in 1841. These mid-19th century changes altered the seating and led to a celebrated row.

As was the custom, the Duke of Hamilton and other landowners had a special gallery for their private use. The burgh council and magistrates were also allocated a gallery, the south-east gallery. After the 1841 renovations, the Duke contested the right of the council and magistrates to use the south-east gallery, presumably because he considered it superior to his own. The issue went to the House of Lords, who found against His Grace.

Return to the main road, turning right for the junction with Brandon Street, behind which is the station. *The distance is about 1¹/₂ miles, plus whatever is clocked up in Strathclyde Park.*

Other attractions in the Hamilton area accessible from the station but not mentioned on the above walk are:

Chatelherault country park

This lies off the A72 Hamilton to Larkhall Road, 1¹/₂ miles from the town centre. As the best walking exists in the park itself, it might be preferable to reach it by bus, from outside the railway station. The park is dominated by the house of Chatelherault, designed by William Adam for James, the fifth Duke, and known colloquially as the Duke of Hamilton's dog kennel! It was used as a hunting lodge and stood on the skyline when viewed from Hamilton Palace, which lay to the west of the Mausoleum and which was demolished in 1922, following mining subsidence. A double avenue of deciduous trees, with an outer avenue of firs, was planted to link the two, and the remains of this can still be seen.

Part of Chatelherault was occupied until the 1960s after which it was the target of vandals, being an empty shell when put up for sale in 1977, with the rest of the High Parks estate, to pay the death duties incurred on the death of the 14th Duke. It has since been painstakingly restored — the plasterwork in the banqueting hall is of particular interest, having been recreated from photographs. All the floors and ceilings are new and much of the carved stonework required replacing. An audio-visual presentation tells the story of the house, while models show what life was like in the 18th century. The gardens are being similarly returned to the way they may have looked, including the *parterre*, a pattern of clipped box hedges.

The house is the focal point of a country park, through which runs the deeply wooded Avon Gorge. There are ten miles of paths which can be wandered at will, one of which follows the route of the

Strathclyde Park

Chatelherault

estate's horse-drawn mineral railway. It is worth seeing the ruins of Cadzow Castle, where Mary Queen of Scots stayed, the earthworks of a possible Iron Age fort and the remains of coal mining, on which the fortunes of the Hamilton family were based. Perhaps the most intriguing link with the past is the small herd of white cattle which live in the park, descendants of the ancient breed which once roamed Cadzow Forest. A ranger service is available. *Details on (0698) 426213.*

Bothwell Castle

Uddingston is the nearest station to this attraction. Walk up to Main Street and turn right. After half a mile turn right into Bellshill Road and left along the right-hand side of the church — NOT down Old Glasgow Road — and continue for about three quarters of a mile until Bothwell Castle car park is reached on the right.

The impressive ruins of Bothwell Castle represent a mixture of construction dates, from the 13th to the 16th centuries. The castle was dismantled at least twice, following capture, and subsequently rebuilt. Towards the end of the 17th century it provided stone for the construction of a mansion house for Archibald Douglas, first Earl of Forfar, who had acquired the castle.

The sequence of deliberate demolition followed by rebuilding has made it difficult for historians to date what remains, but excavations carried out relatively recently have provided firm indications. The castle, as it existed during the Wars of Independence (1296-1357), appears to have been a tower, and it is recorded that the English in 1301 and the Scots in 1337 captured it by the same means — using a belfry, or wooden tower on wheels, from which a drawbridge was dropped onto the top of the fortification.

A number of masons' marks can be seen, and near the well at the basement of the *donjon* the third Duke of Buccleuch carved on the wall a coronet, the initial "B" and the date 1786 (which would indicate that one man's vandalism is another man's historical act). On the rock by the riverside below the south-eastern tower is the inscription: "Clyde rose to this mark, March 12, 1782." This was about 20 feet above ordinary water level and the worst recorded Clyde flood.

Return to Uddingston Station by the same route. *Total distance* $2^1/_2$ *miles.*

Strathclyde Park

The park can be reached from Hamilton Central railway station, as already described, or from Motherwell Station by walking along Muir Street to the crossroads, turning right and continuing along the main road — through a built-up area — for about a mile to the park entrance. Alternatively, it is feasible to walk from one station to the other, via Strathclyde Park, a distance of over two miles. From the walker's point of view, it is perhaps unfortunate that the visitor centre is in the north-west corner of the park, some two miles by the park road from the Hamilton Road, Motherwell, entrance.

Opened in 1978, Strathclyde Country Park occupies 1650 acres in the valley of the River Clyde, and includes open parkland, nature reserves, rough wetland and mature woodland, centred round Strathclyde Loch, and with the River Clyde running through it.

It combines a wide range of sporting activities with outdoor pursuits such as bird-watching and nature trails, with a visitor centre providing displays on what to look for.

The park was created from what was mostly derelict land and the loch is manmade. It was during the construction of the loch in 1973 that earthmoving equip-

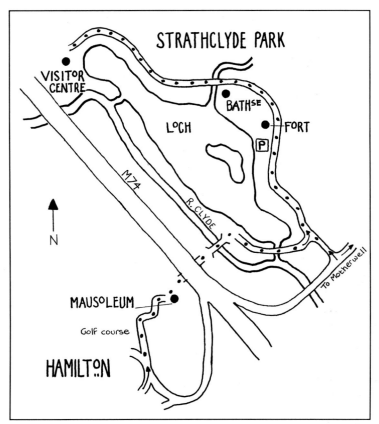

ment revealed quantities of red tile and brick. The significance did not go unrecognised and subsequent investigations established that this was the site of a Roman bathhouse, with four courses of masonry surviving. It has been saved and can be seen by visitors.

On the plateau above the bathhouse stood Bothwellhaugh Roman fort, which was discovered and investigated in the late 1930s. It is thought that the main role of the garrison would be protecting supply trains on the nearby Roman road linking Carlisle with the Antonine Wall. A suggested walk, taking in the Roman interest, begins at the viewpoint car park, which is on the north side of the loch. It includes scrubland consisting mostly of haw-

thorn and birch trees and gorse and broom, supporting a variety of birds and mammals. Take one of the paths on the loch edge, keep left at the first junction and then keep right. After crossing a second wooden bridge, look right towards an area of water occupied by Great Reedmace, a plant with a cigar-shaped head. Continue up the steps and left at the junction, past all the Dog Rose to some steps. At the bottom go right along the South Calder Water.

Pause at the Roman bathhouse then bear right by brambles and hawthorn to the Roman fort car park, then follow the path parallel to the road back to your starting point or to the main gate.

Information on the park is available on (0698) 66155. ❑

Irvine and Kilwinning

These Ayrshire towns, individual in their own rights, are effectively combined administratively with a country park between them

Scottish maritime museum

FROM the station, go through the Irvine Centre shopping mall to Bridgegate, noting the distinctive church buildings on the right as you leave. Turn right into High Street and, after about a quarter of a mile, left into the restored Glasgow Vennel, with the site of Provost Hamilton's house on the corner. Hamilton's son was a medical student friend of the poet Robert Burns and was later a subscriber to Burns' first print. Glasgow Vennel No 4 contains a reconstruction of Burns' bedroom, showing the harsh conditions under which he lived while working in the Heckling Shop from 1781 to 1784, learning the trade of flax dressing. No 10 (the Heckling Shop) is an exhibition centre, with an audio-visual display about the flax-dresing trade and

the recently-restored street. It lasts about 12 minutes. The Buchanite meeting place, on the other side of the street, is privately-owned. Glasgow Vennel is so named because Irvine was once the city's main seaport, with goods transported by cart.

Return to the High Street junction and cross into Kirk Vennel, leading towards Irvine Parish Church, built in 1770 and designed to hold 1770 worshippers, one for every year of Christianity.

Either continue past the graveyard and turn right down the path to a pleasant riverside walk, or make your way through the graveyard to the church then turn left outside the church gates and down to the riverside. Steps on the right lead to the Rivergate shopping mall. Either take these and return to the station or continue along the river bank, crossing by a footbridge, then going under the main road and walking parallel to the railway to reach Fullarton Parish Church. Go under the rail bridge and follow the footpath to Montgomery Street, with its modern corner buildings. The Scottish Maritime Museum is on the right. If you have elected to take the direct route to the station, walking under the railway line will lead you to Montgomery Street.

The museum, centred around the harbour, has a fleet of historic vessels, displays charting the history of seagoing Scotland, and a re-creation of a typical shipyard worker's room and kitchen flat.

Walk around the harbour side to the Magnum Centre, which offers a wide range of leisure activities, and attracts in the region of $1^1/_2$ million visitors a year. Behind the Magnum is Irvine Beach

Park, opened by the Queen in 1979, in which is located the Seaworld Centre. This is the place for close encounters of the maritime kind, with more than 2000 marine creatures in its large tanks.

Return to the station via Montgomery Street. The total distance varies, depending on choice of route and degree of wandering about, but should be around four miles.

The next station to the north, Kilwinning, is the junction of the Glasgow to Ayr and Largs lines. The town contains the ruins of a once-important abbey which can be reached by turning left outside the station into Byres Road to Howgate and through the pedestrian precinct to Abbeygate. The graveyard of the adjacent Abbey Church offers a good view of the abbey, which occupies the site of a Dark Ages settlement.

Outside Kilwinning is Dalgarven Mill, dating from 1620 and the West of Scotland's only productive water mill. The route from the station follows that to the

Glasgow Vennel

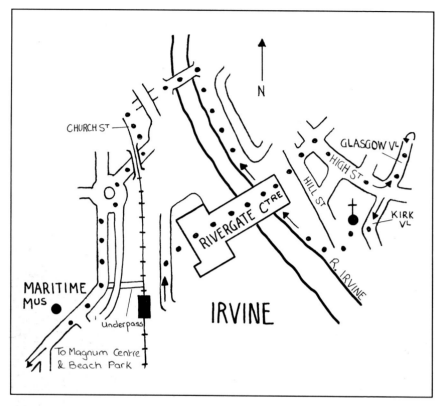

abbey as far as the point at which Byres Road becomes Howgate, where a left turn is required. Follow this road (the A737 to Dalry) for $1^3/_4$ miles to the mill on the right. Here the grain can be traced from ploughing, seeding, harvesting and threshing to the millstones and the bakery. There are also displays of Ayrshire country life and costumes. Either walk back the two miles to Kilwinning station or take a bus. Alternatively, take a bus to Dalry, which also has a railway station.

Between Irvine and Kilwinning is Eglinton Country park, which is probably best accessed by bus from Kilwinning. A visitor centre explains the park's past and natural history and there is a ranger service. *Enquiries to (0294) 51776.*

❑

The Western Islands

Although the Western Islands of Scotland are outside the scope of this book, many of them lie in the Strathclyde region and can be reached with the help of the Day Tripper ticket. This will take you to the ferry terminals at Ardrossan where boats cross to Arran, Largs for the Cumbraes and Wemyss Bay if travelling to Bute. The ferry port for Mull is Oban.

All the ferries listed below are run by Caledonian MacBrayne and usually there's no need to book (see phone details in the Useful Information section).

Cumbrae ferries at Largs

Arran

Arran is often referred to as "Scotland in miniature" offering the visitor a variety of stunning landscapes. From the granite highlands and sweeping moorlands of the north — with Goat Fell towering nearly 3,000 feet into the clouds — to the lusher lowlands and golden sands of the south, the island has something for everyone.

Arran is famous for its geological formations and students come from around the world to study here. It's also rich in prehistoric remains and has Neolithic and early Bronze Age sites. Wildlife abounds — deer roam freely on the hills, seals can be seen basking around the shores and there are said to be more red squirrels here than on any other part of the British Isles. Arran is also a bird spotter's paradise — look out for golden eagles and ptarmigan.

The island offers perfect walking country to suit all tastes and can be cycled round in a day.

Ferry departs Ardrossan. Crossing time 55 minutes.

Bute

Bute is highly cultivated, offering the visitor pleasant woodland and gently undulating countryside. The northern tip is enclosed by the Cowal peninsula and the southern end marked by St Blane's Hill and the rocky coastline below. The most notable attraction on the island, and well worth visiting, is Rothesay Castle which is open to the public daily. Rothesay, the island's capital, also has a fine harbour, winter gardens plus all the usual facilities of a popular holiday resort.

Ferry departs Wemyss Bay. Crossing time 30 minutes.

The Cumbraes

These two small islands lie in between the mainland and the island of Bute, approximately one mile west of Largs.

Great Cumbrae — it is actually only four miles by two — has a rocky coastline with low cliffs. There are excellent views of Arran and the mainland from the island. The holiday resort of Millport on the southern tip offers plenty of facilities for the holidaymaker, and you can also hire a bicycle from here for a leisurely cycle around the island.

The privately-owned, Little Cumbrae, lies half a mile to the south.

Ferry departs Largs to Cumbrae Slip. Crossing time 10 minutes.

Islay

This, the most southerly of the Inner Hebrides, boasts mile upon mile of white sandy beaches and, like Arran, a varied landscape. The island offers particularly good bird watching country with around 250 species recorded. Prehistoric remains can be found all over the island. There is an 18-hole golf course at Machrie, craft centres, a museum and several distilleries producing famous malt whiskies.

Ferry departs Kennacraig on Kintyre. Crossing time 2 hours 20 minutes.

Port Askaig on Islay — ferry port for Jura and the mainland service

Oban-bound SuperSprinter pictured near Connel on Loch Etive

Jura

Most of Jura is an empty waste of trackless moor and mountain but the island has a rugged beauty which many will find irresistible. In its favour is a mild climate, soaring hills from which magnificent views can be obtained (you can see Ireland and the Isle of Man on a clear day) and plentiful wildlife, including wild deer and goats and many bird species. Indeed, the name Jura comes from the Norse *Dyr Oe* meaning deer island. The island's small population all live on the east coast, and most of these around the harbour town of Craighouse which has two piers, one of which was built by Thomas Telford. Another famous name connected with the island is George Orwell who wrote his famous novel, *1984*, while staying in a cottage in the north.

The island can be reach by a short ferry crossing from Port Askaig on Islay

Mull

The island of Mull, the third largest in the Hebrides, offers spectacular coastal scenery, high hills and many places of interest. It also boasts the only passenger-carrying miniature railway in the West Highlands — thousands of people make the 20-minute trip from Craignure on the east of the island, to the line's end at Torosay Castle. The ride gives splendid views of the Sound of Mull and Ben Nevis, Loch Linnhe and the Glencoe mountain range on the mainland.

Torosay is one of many romantic castles on the island and one which is still lived in. It has a 12-acre garden with an Italian statue walk, terraces, and water and Japanese gardens.

With its sandy beaches, cliffs, mountains, peat bogs, woodlands and forests, the island has one of the most varied habitats in the British Isles. Wildlife includes red and roe deer, golden eagle and the very rare sea eagle, seals and, off the coast, killer whales.

Main ferry from Oban to Craignure. Crossing time 40 minutes.

Iona and Staffa

Lying off the western shores of Mull and only a short ferry crossing away are Iona with its ancient abbey and, a little to the north, Staffa and its spectacular rock formations including Fingal's cave, which inspired the composer Mendelssohn.

Iona tends to get inundated with visitors during the holiday season, but most never stray further than the main tourist spots. The west coast, on the other hand, with its crofting community, secluded bays and sandy beaches are left untouched.

Boat trips run to Staffa from Oban, Ulva

Ferry and Fionnphort on Mull, and Iona. A ferry links Fionnphort with Iona. In the summer there are through bus and steamer connections to Fionnphort via Craignure to and from Oban. Crossing time from Mull to Iona 10 minutes. ❏

Right: Torosay terminus of the Mull railway

TOROSAY CASTLE & GARDENS

Isle of Mull

Visit a homely Victorian Castle set in 12 acres of varied but consistently peaceful gardens travelling by 10 inch gauge railway from Craignure, a mile and a half distant — steam and diesel hauled. Tel: 06802 421

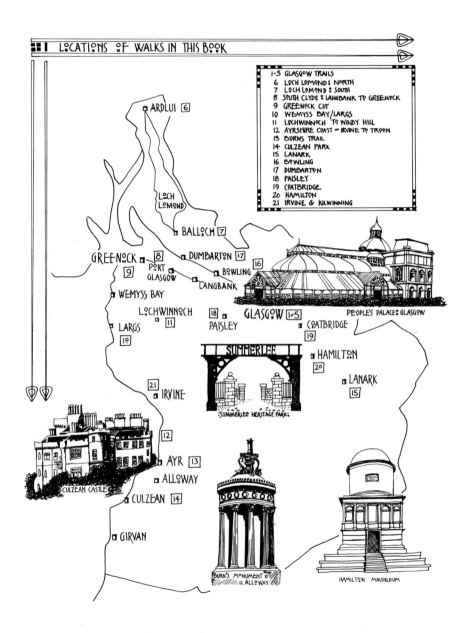

LOCATIONS OF WALKS IN THIS BOOK

1-5 GLASGOW TRAILS
6 LOCH LOMOND : NORTH
7 LOCH LOMOND : SOUTH
8 SOUTH CLYDE : LANGBANK TO GREENOCK
9 GREENOCK CUT
10 WEMYSS BAY/LARGS
11 LOCHWINNOCH TO WINDY HILL
12 AYRSHIRE COAST - IRVINE TO TROON
13 BURNS TRAIL
14 CULZEAN PARK
15 LANARK
16 BOWLING
17 DUMBARTON
18 PAISLEY
19 COATBRIDGE
20 HAMILTON
21 IRVINE & KILWINNING

ARDLUI 6

LOCH LOMOND

BALLOCH 7

GREENOCK 8   DUMBARTON 17
PORT 9   BOWLING 16
GLASGOW   LANGBANK

WEMYSS BAY

LOCHWINNOCH 11   18 GLASGOW 1-5
PAISLEY   PEOPLE'S PALACE : GLASGOW

LARGS 10   COATBRIDGE 19

SUMMERLEE   HAMILTON 20

21 IRVINE   LANARK 15

SUMMERLEE HERITAGE PARK

12   AYR 13

CULZEAN CASTLE   ALLOWAY

CULZEAN 14

GIRVAN

BURNS MONUMENT
ALLOWAY

HAMILTON MAUSOLEUM

Useful information

TRANSPORT ENQUIRIES

ScotRail passenger enquiries: 041 204 2844
Strathclyde Transport enquiries: 041 226 4826.
Glasgow Buchanan Street bus station: 041 332 7133/9191
Glasgow Anderston bus station: 041 248 7432
Western Scottish Omnibuses: 0563 22551
Caledonian MacBrayne (main office, Gourock): 0475 33755; Oban: 0631 62285
Countess Fiona (Loch Lomond cruising): 0389 52044
PS Waverley excursions: 041 221 8152
Clyde river cruises: 041 221 8702

TOURIST BOARDS

Scottish Tourist Board, 23 Ravelston Terrace, Edinburgh EH4 3EU: 031 332 2433.
Greater Glasgow Tourist Board, 35 St Vincent Place, Glasgow G1 2ER: 041 227 4880.
Town Hall, Abbey Close, Paisley PA1 1JS: 041 889 0711.
Inverclyde Information Centre, Municipal Buildings, Greenock PA15 1LQ:
0475 24400
Clyde Valley Tourist Board, Horsemarket, Ladyacre Road, Lanark ML11 7LQ:
0555 2544.
Ayr and Burns Country Tourist Board, 39 Sandgate, Ayr: 0292 284196.
Ayrshire Valleys Tourist Board, 62 Bank Street, Kilmarnock KA1 1ER: 0563 39090.
Cunninghame District Council Department of Leisure, Recreation and Tourism,
Greenock Road, Largs, KA30 8BG: 0475 673765.
Oban, Mull and District Tourist Board, Albany Street, Oban PA34 4AN: 0631 63122
Mid-Argyll, Kintyre and Islay Tourist Board, The Pier, Campbeltown, Argyll PA28
6EF: 0586 52056
Dunoon and Cowal Tourist Board, 7 Alexandra Parade, Dunoon, PA23 8AB: 0369
3755
Isle of Arran Tourist Board, The Pier, Brodick, Arran KA27 8AU: 0770 2140
Isle of Bute Tourist Board, The Pier, Rothesay, Bute, PA20 9AQ: 0700 2151
Loch Lomond, Stirling and Trossachs Tourist Board, 41 Dumbarton Road, Stirling,
FK8 2LQ: 0786 75019

MUSEUMS AND ART GALLERIES

Art Galleries, Kelvingrove, Glasgow: 041 357 3929
Burns Cottage, Alloway, near Ayr: 0292 41215
Burrell Gallery, Pollok Country Park, Pollokshaws Road, Glasgow: 041 649 7151
Cameronian Museum, Mote Hill, off Muir Street, Hamilton: 0698 428688
Haggs Castle, 100 St Andrews Drive, Glasgow: 041 427 2725
Hamilton District Museum, 129 Muir Street: 0698 283981
Heckling Shop and Glasgow Vennel, Irvine: 0294 75059

Kelvingrove art galleries, Glasgow

Hunterian Art Gallery, University of Glasgow: 041 330 5431
Hunterian Museum, University of Glasgow: 041 330 4421
Largs Museum, Kirkgate House, Manse Court: 0475 687081
McLean Museum and Art Gallery, 5 Kelly Street, Greenock: 0475 23741
McLellan Galleries, 270 Sauchiehall Street, Glasgow: 041 332 1132
McLaurin Gallery, Rozelle Estate, Alloway: 0292 45447
Paisley Museum and Art Galleries, High Street: 041 889 3151
People's Palace, Glasgow Green, Glasgow: 041 554 0223
Pollok House, Pollok Country Park, Pollokshaws Road, Glasgow: 041 632 0274
Provand's Lordship, 3 Castle Street, Glasgow: 041 552 8819
Regimental Museum of the Royal Highland Fusiliers, 518 Sauchiehall Street, Glasgow: 041 332 0961
Scottish Maritime Museum, Irvine: 0294 78283.
Denny ship model tank, Dumbarton: 0389 63444
Springburn Museum, Atlas Square, Ayr Street, Glasgow: 041 557 1405
Summerlee Heritage Park, West Canal Street, Coatbridge: 0236 31261
Tenement House, 145 Buccleuch Street, Glasgow: 041 333 0183
Third Eye Centre, 350 Sauchiehall Street, Glasgow: 041 332 7521
Transport Museum, 1 Bunhouse Road, Glasgow: 041 357 3929

CHARLES RENNIE MACKINTOSH

Queen's Cross Church (headquarters of the Charles Rennie
Mackintosh Society), 870 Garscube Road, Glasgow: 041 946 6600

Glasgow School of Art, 167 Renfrew Street: 041 332 9797
Hunterian Art Gallery, University of Glasgow: 041 330 5431
Scotland Street School, Scotland Street, Glasgow: 041 429 1202
Willow Tearooms, 217 Sauchiehall Street, Glasgow: 041 332 0521
Ruchill Church Hall, Ruchill Street, Glasgow: 041 946 0466
Martyr's School, Barony Street, Townhead, Glasgow: 041 552 2104
Kelvingrove Art Gallery, Glasgow: 041 357 3929
The Hill House, Upper Colquhoun Street, Helensburgh: 0436 73900

COUNTRY PARKS

Balloch Castle: 0389 58216
Chatelherault, Hamilton: 0698 426213
Culzean: 06556 274
Drumpellier, Coatbridge: 0236 22257
Eglinton, Irvine: 0294 51776
Finlaystone, Langbank: 047554 285
Kelburn, Largs: 0475 568685
Pollok, Glasgow: 041 632 9299
Strathclyde, Motherwell/Hamilton: 0698 66155

Trams at Summerlee heritage park, Coatbridge

VISITOR CENTRES

Dalgarven Mill, Kilwinning: 0294 52448
David Livingstone Centre, Blantyre: 0698 823140
Land O' Burns Centre, Alloway, near Ayr: 0292 43700
Lochwinnoch RSPB: 0505 842663
New Lanark: 0555 65876 (conservation village); 0555 65262 (Scottish Wildlife Trust)
University of Glasgow, University Avenue, Hillhead, Glasgow: 041 330 5511

OTHER ATTRACTIONS:

City Chambers, George Square, Glasgow: 041 221 9600
Coats Observatory, Oakshaw Street, Paisley: 041 889 3151
Hutcheson's Hall, 158 Ingram Street, Glasgow (regional headquarters of the National Trust for Scotland): 041 552 8391
Magnum Centre, Harbourside, Irvine: 0294 78381
Mitchell Library, North Street, Glasgow: 041 221 7030
Paisley Abbey, Abbey Close, Paisley: 041 889 3630
Seaworld, Beach Park, Irvine: 0294 311414

Acknowledgements

Leading Edge would like to thank Strathclyde Passenger Transport Executive for its help in the production of this book.

The publisher is also grateful to the following for their help with photographs and illustrations:

David & Charles: p12

Museum of Transport, Glasgow: pp13, 27

ScotRail: p33

National Trust for Scotland: p48

Greater Glasgow Tourist Board and Convention Bureau: p59

Springburn Museum: p 66 © Mitchell Library

Loch Lomond, Stirling & Trossachs Tourist Board: pp71, 78

Inverclyde District Libraries: p75

Eric Thorburn/Cunninghame District Council: p81

Roger Smith: pp83, 86, 87, 89, 90, 91

Clyde Valley Tourist Board: pp103, 106, 125, 127

Renfrew District Council: p118

All other photography by Tom Noble

Mail order books from Leading Edge

Other titles on the **RailTrail** theme

The Isle of Man by Tram, Train and Foot — *Stan Basnett and David Freke*, £4.95

The Great Metro Guide to Tyne and Wear — *Vernon Abbott and Roy Chapman*, £5.95

Settle & Carlisle Country, featuring a new walkers' and cyclists' route from Leeds to Carlisle — *Colin Speakman and John Morrison*, £5.95

Pennine Rails and Trails, exploring Calderdale and Rochdale by train and foot — *John Morrison and Lydia Speakman*, £5.75

Buxton Spa Rail Rambles — *Les Lumsdon and Martin Smith*, 99p

Stockton on Tees: Birthplace of Railways — *Lydia Speakman and Roy Chapman*, £1.95

Other railway books

The Line that Refused to Die — *Stan Abbott and Alan Whitehouse tell the story of the successful campaign to save the Settle & Carlisle line. Features a foreword by Michael Palin.* £6.25 in paperback. Commemorative hardback edition, £13.50.

The Wensleydale Railway — *Christine Hallas*, £3.25

To Kill a Railway — *Stan Abbott's historic account of British Rail's attempts to close the Settle & Carlisle line*, £3.95

Other outdoor books

The Off-Road Bicycle Book. *Second edition of Iain Lynn's authoritative run-down on mountain biking*, £4.95

The Birds of Lincolnshire and South Humberside — *Stephen Lorand and Keith Atkin*, £12.50

Brick by Brick, *guide to building your own home*, £6.25

All available from your bookshop or direct from —
Leading Edge, Old Chapel, Burtersett, Hawes, North Yorkshire, DL8 3PB.
Use our telephone credit card ordering service, or write or phone for our up-to-date catalogue.
Postage and packing charges — books under £2, add 35p; over £2, add 75p; over £10, add £1.

☎ (0969) 667566

144